Tax, Justice, and Society

Tax, Justice, and Society

Authors:

Austin Mardon

Abdulrahman Aldada

Anushka Hasija

Bilal Ahmed

Brett Fawcett

Daivat Bhavsar

Daniel Klassen

Erwin Kwok

Ivan Frimpong

Jaime Johnson

John Christy Johnson

Julia Cara

Lea Touliopoulos

Monsur Moshood

Mya George

Peter Anto Johnson

Editor:
Catherine Mardon

Published by Golden Meteorite Press

Golden Meteorite Press

103 11919 82 St NW

Edmonton, AB T5B 2W3

www.goldenmeteoritepress.com

ISBN: 978-1-77369-886-1

EBook ISBN: 978-1-77369-887-8

GM

PRESS

Typeset and Cover Design by Nadia Feller

Table of Contents

Introduction

In this book, we take an in-depth look at tax, justice, and society. Governments at the municipal, provincial, and federal levels have developed systems or have looked into how we can create a more "just" society. The following chapters are individually focused on those systems or aspects of those systems to provide a comprehensive overview of the public policies of tax or redistribution. In the course of doing so, a definition of what "just" means is provided. We review the facets of these policies in terms of social, political, ethical, and philosophical implications of certain changes to society. Examples include contentions such as taxing the wealthy at a higher level, and providing everyone a basic income regardless of their willingness to contribute to the labour market.

Many issues are examined within each chapter. Relating to these issues, important questions raised include how people should be taxed and how much they should be paying in taxes. The effects of globalization on the tax burden of the middle class are also discussed given recent social developments. For instance, advocacy on tax justice is a topic given the increase in corporations, businesses, and even individuals finding clever ways to avoid paying taxes like by using shell companies in offshore accounts. Interlinked between all the book's topics is their underlying focus on moral philosophy. Specifically, as a means to answer whether or not owning private property can be considered theft and a framework to understand the social implications of taxation. Other questions we consider include whether just deserts are obtained through personal efforts or based on need and what should be considered ethical or acceptable according to the subjective views of members of society. In delving into these topics, important debates about gender, race, and cultural inequality are reviewed. We also engage controversial subjects such as universal basic income and whether or not becoming billionaires and accruing wealth should be possible. Join us as we explore tax principles to understand how a "just" society is created.

Criteria and Overview of Tax Equity

Introduction

Tax justice has become a highly popularized topic in recent years, given how global economies have been straying further away from equitable tax distribution. This chapter examines tax justice and fairness, why it is important (i.e., the injustices that currently exist such as tax havens), several theories on how taxes should be structured, and lastly discuss current strides being made towards tax justice.

What is Tax Justice?

Tax justice describes policies and theories aiming for the establishment of equity through fair taxes, especially for the wealthy and multinational corporations ("What is tax justice?", n.d.). It typically focuses on finding and denouncing injustices such as tax havens, corruption, and tax avoidance or abuse by multinational corporations and the extremely wealthy. The principle of tax fairness mandates that the total tax burden should be distributed and divided fairly amongst the tax-paying population (Dodge, 2005).

Globalization and Tax Injustice

Tax justice is of extreme relevance and significance in today's world. Namely, in recent years, the push towards globalization has created new injustices in the form of inequitable tax distribution. The middle classes living in developed countries have seen large increases in taxation, which has not been matched by increases in wages, thus presenting the danger of downward social mobility. In essence, globalization has increased the tax burden on the middle classes and reduced it on the wealthy and large corporations (Zacharie, 2019). Specifically, globalization has allowed companies to become more mobile across different countries and engage in foreign investment. To attract investments, governments have been lowering corporate tax rates dramatically to outcompete other nations' governments. This can be seen in various statistics -- for example, in Europe, the average corporate tax rate fell from 35% in 1995 to a mere 22% in 2018. In the USA, under the Trump administration, the corporate tax rate decreased in 2017 from 35 to 21%. On average, corporate tax rates worldwide have decreased dramatically, falling from an average of more than 40% to less than 25% between 1980 and 2015 (Zacharie, 2019).

Aside from corporations, personal income tax rates on the wealthiest members of society have also made a downward trend in recent years. In the Organization for Economic Cooperation and Development (OECD), which comprises 38 member countries, the top marginal tax rate decreased by an average of 40% between 1981 and 2017 (Zacharie, 2019). This trend is mirrored in several countries, especially when far right-wing political leaders come into power (e.g. the Reagan administration in the US, and the Thatcher administration in the UK). All in all, to offset the decrease in revenue caused by the reduced corporate and top personal income tax rates, governments have increased tax rates on the middle class (Zacharie, 2019).

These tax inequalities are only exacerbated by tax evasion and avoidance strategies employed by large corporations and wealthy individuals. These strategies essentially take advantage of loopholes to minimize their tax rates, resulting in a larger burden on the government and on middle and lower-class individuals. Tax evasion strategies by the richest 1% are estimated to cost US$200 billion annually (Zacharie, 2019). An example of a tax avoidance strategy is tax havens, which will be discussed in the section below.

Tax Havens

Often referred to as offshore financial centers, "tax havens" are countries or regions with minimal to no corporate tax (Fitzgibbon & Hallman, 2020). These low corporate taxes thus attract foreign investors, allowing outsiders (which are typically large companies and the richest individuals) to transfer their assets and set up businesses in these havens to avoid getting taxed at a higher rate in their home countries. Additionally, offshore financial centers are often very private and highly limit the amount of information that is available to the public about these companies. Tax havens typically deny even being tax havens (Fitzgibbon & Hallman, 2020). These havens are located in several places globally, including countries such as Panama, the Netherlands, and Malta, and regions such as the US state of Delaware. There are several shocking statistics regarding tax havens and the massive finances they hold -- it is estimated that tax havens hold up to US$5.6 trillion in financial assets, which amounts to roughly a whopping 10% of the entire globe's GDP (Zacharie, 2019). As a result, governments are estimated to lose more than $800 billion in revenue every year (Fitzgibbon & Hallman, 2020). Of these financial assets, 80% are owned by the richest 0.1%. Put another way, 50% of these financial assets are owned by the richest 0.01% (Zacharie, 2019)! Approximately 40% of annual corporate profits are transferred to tax havens, to avoid having to pay massive taxes on these profits (Fitzgibbon & Hallman, 2020).

Tax havens are exacerbating several tax inequality issues, hence the strong fight against them. Intergenerational wealth and "old money" are kept alive through cycles of wealthy people keeping their funds in tax havens, essentially widening the gap between the rich and poor. Large corporations, on the other hand, save extra revenue from not having to pay high corporate taxes and can use it to give shareholders higher dividends and outcompete smaller companies. The total GDP lost due to tax havens is much higher in smaller, developing countries which also need the tax revenue much more, thus again worsening inequalities between the rich and the poor (Fitzgibbon & Hallman, 2020).

Several companies and individuals opt to set up 'shell companies in tax havens. A shell company is a 'company' that typically only exists on paper, with no physical office space or employees, created in a tax haven. For example, a single office building in the Cayman Islands, another notable tax haven, houses approximately 19,000 shell companies (Fitzgibbon & Hallman, 2020). Shell companies can hold several assets, including money, luxury houses, intellectual property, businesses, and many more. Tax havens are very beneficial to those who use them, both individuals and companies. Individuals typically use shell companies for purposes of concealing their transactions, making it more difficult for people such as ex-spouses, ex-business partners, or tax inspectors to track money owed. As mentioned previously, businesses make huge profits in tax savings by transferring funds and investments into offshore financial centers via subsidiaries (a subsidiary is essentially a 'daughter' company to a 'parent' company, enabling the parent company to deposit their money into a tax haven through the daughter company) (Chen, 2020). These large corporations save over $500 billion in taxes using tax avoidance strategies every year (Fitzgibbon & Hallman, 2020)!

Why Tax Justice is Important

By fighting for tax justice on a global scale, inequities like these would be adequately addressed. Further, by eliminating injustices like tax havens and shell companies, governments would be able to use this revenue towards public goods and services. To restore the balance of tax burden distribution, it is necessary to tax all people at the same progressive rate, and the top marginal rate of tax should also be increased (Zacharie, 2019). Fraudulent activity in offshore companies and tax havens must further be targeted, possibly by establishing a public register of the true beneficiaries of large companies and tracking the countries where these companies conduct business or transfer funds. To address the competition between governments trying to offer the lowest corporate tax rates possible, a global minimum corporate tax rate should be introduced. This levels the playing ground and mandates that all corporations must pay a certain amount to operate in any given country, thus lifting some of the tax burdens off of the middle and lower classes (Zacharie, 2019).

While there is an effort to address these injustices and move the world towards equitable tax distribution within councils such as the European Union and the OECD, there is still a long way to go. Citizens must be educated and informed on the injustices occurring and form movements to lobby policymakers to fix these issues (Zacharie, 2019).

How Should Taxes Be Structured?

There are various theories as to how taxes should be structured. Traditional theories of tax justice include the old benefit principle of tax fairness, as well as vertical and horizontal equity. Newer theories include the new benefit principle, the cost-of-service principle, the objective approach of the ability to pay principle, and more. While several countries have trended towards income tax systems in recent years, there is still debate on whether taxes should be structured based on consumption or income tax. The following section will delve deeper into these theories.

Vertical and horizontal equity

According to the book The Myth of Ownership: Taxes and Justice by Liam Murphy and Thomas Nagel, "traditional analyses of tax justice demand that the distribution of tax burdens satisfies criteria of vertical and horizontal equity" (2004). To satisfy these demands, we first must define what vertical and horizontal equity are. Horizontal equity argues that individuals with equal incomes should pay equal amounts of tax ("A Defense of Horizontal and Vertical Equity in Taxation", n.d.). Furthermore, vertical equity argues that taxes should be proportional to income, in that individuals with higher incomes should pay higher taxes than those with lower incomes. This is the concept of progressive taxation ("A Defense of Horizontal and Vertical Equity in Taxation", n.d.). Progressive taxation is the traditional definition by which many countries and policies model their tax justice systems after. However, in recent years there has been debate as to whether horizontal and vertical equity is the best way to distribute tax burdens in society. Various alternative structures and theories have been proposed.

Old and new benefit principle of tax fairness

This principle is based on how much you receive from the government and argues that you should contribute accordingly (Dodge, 2005). This was, however, critiqued because it is often hard to directly measure benefits received by the government, and when someone is on welfare it is illogical to maintain the contribution principle. The new benefit principle is another

14

principle that operates on the same basis of paying taxes based on benefit. However, it addresses the issues that the old benefit principle was critiqued for. Essentially, the new principle considers a taxpayer's economic well-being as a way to measure benefits received by the government. It also prioritizes income tax much higher than consumption tax (Dodge, 2005).

Consumption tax vs income tax

Consumption tax is defined as the taxes incurred when you buy a good or service (Kagan, 2021). Some examples of this taxation include sales taxes, tariffs, excise taxes (e.g., taxes on alcohol and tobacco), etc. Aside from this, consumption tax can also refer to an actual tax burden distribution theory wherein people are taxed based on how much they consume or "take away" from the economy. This second definition of consumption tax used to be the national system in the US. However, it has since been replaced with income tax (Kagan, 2021). Nonetheless, there are still several countries throughout the globe such as Japan that employs a national consumption tax. The rationale behind this is to encourage saving and discourage excess spending.

As the essential principle behind consumption tax is to reward savers and penalize spenders, proponents of consumption tax claim that by encouraging people to save, consumption tax promotes investment, thereby strengthening the economy (Kagan, 2021). Additionally, proponents of consumption tax argue that income tax does just the opposite by penalizing savers and rewarding spenders and that people should not be taxed based on what they earn, or in other words, contribute to society. Rather, they should be taxed on how much they take away. Conversely, opponents of consumption tax claim that it is a form of regressive taxation that unfairly targets the poor. The nationwide consumption tax is typically a fixed percentage; wealthier people have to provide a smaller fraction of their income to pay their taxes while poorer people must spend more of their income (Kagan, 2021).

Cost of service principle

The government incurs costs to provide various services and public goods to its citizens, and this theory argues that citizens should pay taxes determined in part by the cost of operation of these public goods and services (Chand, 2014). As a result, taxes are virtually treated as the 'price' of these public goods and services. Opponents of this principle argue that it is hard to calculate the cost of public goods and services, as well as how much of a public good or service a taxpayer is receiving. Additionally, this theory of taxation is "quid pro quo", meaning a favour for a favour (i.e., exchanging goods or services that are equivalent in value to one another). This goes against the basic purpose of taxation - tax is not a price or cost. Lastly, welfare is nonexistent with this theory - the government would be unable to provide public goods such as free education to the poorest members of society, as they likely would not be able to pay for it (Chand, 2014).

Benefit principle

Although this theory was briefly discussed above, in both its old and new principles, this section will examine it in much more detail. As aforementioned, this theory operates on the basis that taxes should be paid by the benefits that taxpayers receive from the government (i.e., through social goods or services) (Chand, 2014). Essentially, those who enjoy more benefits from the government (i.e., obtain more utility from public goods) should pay higher taxes. There are, however, cons to this principle as well. Again, like the cost of service principle, this theory is "quid pro quo", which goes against the rationale behind taxation. It can be thought of as a form of regressive taxation if applied literally. For example, a poor person would likely receive a lot of government assistance (e.g. subsidization of housing). Since they are enjoying more benefits from the government, based on this principle they should pay more in taxes - this is unfair, as the poor person likely would not be able to pay higher taxes. Often, the point of social goods and services provided by the government is to assist the poor who perhaps would not otherwise be able to afford such goods (i.e., welfare). This principle goes against this very rationale (Chand, 2014).

The objective approach of ability to pay principle

This theory measures each taxpayer's taxable capacity, which takes into account many factors such as income, overall wealth and assets, consumption, etc. (Chand, 2014). Other more specific factors that are considered include how income is earned, sources of wealth (i.e. through savings or inheritance), and more. In essence, this theory tries to minimize the subjectivity seen in the previous two principles and attempts to focus on the taxpayer rather than what the taxpayer receives. Despite this, there is still some arbitrariness when it comes to determining someone's taxability with this principle (Chand, 2014).

Taxable capacity

This term refers to "the minimum tax which might be collected from a particular taxpayer or a group of taxpayers" (Chand, 2014). Essentially, it focuses on how much taxpayers can pay. Recently, the definition of taxable capacity has changed to mean the maximum amount that a given taxpayer can pay instead. Due to increasing public expenditures and high welfare costs being incurred by the government, taxable capacity now means how much someone can pay in taxes without adversely affecting their economic well-being. Thus, if you go over the taxable capacity ceiling, it is considered over-taxation. This principle, however, still does not come without its difficulties. Setting a practical definition of taxable capacity is a difficult practice, as how taxable capacity can be determined and what is to be measured as part of it are all subject to debate (Chand, 2014).

Which system is 'best'?

There is a great deal of debate surrounding which tax system is the best (i.e., progressive taxation, which aligns with vertical equity, versus flat taxation, where everyone is charged the same tax rate as is the case with a consumption tax, versus regressive taxation, where those with lower incomes pay higher tax rates than those with higher incomes, etc.). Many countries, however, favour a progressive income tax as they argue it is one of the fairer taxation systems which minimizes the burden on low-income individuals. Progressive income tax systems can often be created under the 'taxable capacity' principle, on a broader scale which applies to all of society rather than examining each individual's taxable capacity.

Strides Towards Tax Justice Today

Some groups and organizations have been formed in the interest of exposing tax injustices in our global society and advocating for tax justice; namely, the Tax Justice Network, Canadians for Tax Fairness, Global Tax Justice, and the Global Alliance for Tax Justice. The Tax Justice Network (TJN) has estimated that cross-border tax evasion activity in a single year amounts to enough money to vaccinate the entire world's population, more than three times ("The State of Tax Justice 2021", 2022). Additionally, the TJN emphasizes that while

18

higher-income countries lose more absolute money in tax revenues, lower incomes lose more relatively in tax revenues, as the tax lost represents a greater percentage of their GDP and GNP ("The State of Tax Justice 2021", 2022). In addition to conducting extensive research on tax revenue lost to evasion and avoidance strategies, the TJN also publishes annual reports on the regions of the world that are most complicit in helping multinational corporations avoid paying the full extent of their taxes. These annual reports are known as the Corporate Tax Haven Index (CTHI), and country profiles have also been published to examine each country's role in global tax evasion strategies in further detail ("Corporate Tax Haven Index - 2021 Results, 2022). In 2021, the top 5 countries with the highest CTHI value (meaning the countries contributing to tax avoidance the most) were: the British Virgin Islands, the Cayman Islands, Bermuda, the Netherlands, and Switzerland, with all of the first 3 jurisdictions having a reportedly "unrestrained scope" on how much corporate tax abuse their financial systems allow ("Corporate Tax Haven Index - 2021 Results, 2022).

In their 2021 report, the TJN took a focus on the financial consequences of the COVID-19 pandemic, urging for a reworking of international tax system rules to collect more tax revenues from multinational corporations to help finance the costs incurred by governments during the pandemic (e.g., testing, vaccination) ("The State of Tax Justice 2021", 2022). In their proposals, they featured both short-term and long-term plans for changing these rules. In the short term, the TJN advocated for a "pandemic excess profits tax" on multinational corporations, and in the long term, they advocated for the establishment of a constant universal tax rate on these corporations. They also urged for increased transparency regarding taxation and the routing of payments to tax havens and other subsidiaries. Lastly, they recommended the UN host negotiations about international tax rules to provide representation for poorer countries ("The State of Tax Justice 2021", 2022).

Conclusion

Overall, tax justice is a highly polarizing topic when it comes to the divide between the wealthiest and poorest in society. While several countries have implemented progressive taxation systems which ideally should minimize the burden of taxes on the poorest, there is an enormous amount of underground activity employed by wealthy individuals and large corporations through which huge portions of tax payments are avoided. Additionally, while they have implemented progressive tax systems, in the age of globalization many countries have also begun to operate in the best interest of their economy to attract foreign investment. Thus, they have lowered their corporate tax rates and highest individual tax rates, which essentially goes against the purpose of tax fairness and progressive taxation. While there have been several movements and groups founded to advocate for tax justice, there is still a long way to go. Transparency should be maximized to illuminate the true extent of the tax avoidance occurring every year, allowing citizens to gain knowledge on this issue and hopefully fight back.

References

Chand, S. (2014, February 17). Theories of equitable distribution of tax burden. Your Article Library. Retrieved from https://www.yourarticlelibrary.com/tax/theories-of-equitable-distribution-of-tax-burden/26283

Chen, J. (2020, September 29). Subsidiary company: Definition, example, and how it works. Investopedia. Retrieved from https://www.investopedia.com/terms/s/subsidiary.asp

Dodge, J. M. (2005). Theories of Tax Justice: Ruminations on the Benefit, Partnership, and Ability-to-Pay Principles. Social Science Research Network. Retrieved from https://papers.ssrn.com/sol3/papers.cfm?abstract_id=696821

European Union. (2022, April 15). The State of Tax Justice 2021. EU Tax Observatory. Retrieved from https://www.taxobservatory.eu/repository/the-state-of-tax-justice-2021/

Fitzgibbon, W., & Hallman, B. (2020, April 6). What is a tax haven? Offshore Finance, explained. International Consortium of Investigative Journalists. Retrieved from https://www.icij.org/investigations/panama-papers/what-is-a-tax-haven-offshore-finance-explained/

Kagan, J. (2021, November 31). Consumption tax explained: Definition, types, vs. income tax. Investopedia. Retrieved from https://www.investopedia.com/terms/c/consumption-tax.asp

Lindsay, I. (2014). A Defense of Horizontal and Vertical Equity in Taxation. Michigan Law. Retrieved from https://www.law.umich.edu/events/junior-scholars-conference/Documents/A%20Defense%20of%20Horizontal%20and%20Vertical%20Equity%20in%20Taxation%20Abstract%20UMich%20-%20Ira%20Lindsay.pdf.

Murphy, L. & Nagel, T. (2004). Traditional Criteria of Tax Equity. The Myth of Ownership: Taxes and Justice (New York, 2002; online edn, Oxford Academic), doi: 10.1093/0195150163.003.0002

Roleplay. (n.d.). What is tax justice? Tax Justice Network. Retrieved from https://taxjustice.net/faq/what-is-tax-justice/

Tax Justice Network. (2022). Corporate Tax Haven Index - 2021 Results. Corporate Tax Haven Index. Retrieved from https://cthi.taxjustice.net/en/cthi/cthi-2021-results

Zacharie, A. (2019, October 3). Why the fight for Tax Justice is a global struggle. Equal Times. Retrieved from https://www.equaltimes.org/why-the-fight-for-tax-justice-is-a?lang=en#.Y41wquzMLlx

Moral and Economic Theories of Private Property

Introduction

Economics, as a discipline, arguably strives to be amoral to-day. This does not mean that economists themselves are immoral, or personally lack any sense of morality. However, modern notions of scientific objectivity (and the "physics envy" that those in the so-called "soft sciences" sometimes feel) preclude moral considerations, since science is (we are told) meant to be purely descriptive, not prescriptive. If Heisenberg says that the more accurately a particle's position can be determined, the less accurately its momentum can be predicted, he does not add that the particle is behaving mischievously or immorally by being deceitful, or that we ought not to imitate the particle in our daily lives. In the same way, an economist might say, the Laffer curve is not setting out to say what the morally correct tax rate is; it is simply attempting to pinpoint which tax rate will garner the state the most revenue. How much tax it is ethical to collect is, we are told, beyond economics' purview. Perhaps it is no wonder it has been known since Carlyle as "the dismal science" (Carlyle, 1849).

But, in the past, economics was recognized as being part of moral philosophy, or at least intimately intertwined with it. It is not a coincidence that Adam Smith was originally known as a moral philosopher and that his most significant work besides The Wealth of Nations was The Theory of Moral Sentiments. Moreover, treating morality as a "non-scientific" question is, in a sense, to say that morality is something unreal, or at least not objectively ascertainable. For the sake of this article, let's grant the possibility that we can talk about moral reality a little more objectively than we can talk about which brand of peanut butter tastes the best.

An obvious example of where this would be valuable is tax policy. Is it true, as the slogan asserts, that "taxation is theft"? This libertarian sentiment makes a positive assertion about what tax policy should be based on certain moral ideas about economics, specifically the idea of private property.

What is especially interesting is that this maxim has the same structure as the socialist anarchist economist Pierre-Joseph Proudhon's famous quote that "property is theft." For Proudhon, the government taking your private property is not theft; rather, you owning private property at all is a form of theft, since you are taking away from the community access to something that properly belongs to it (Proudhon, 1859).

The empirical data on the supply-demand models, with their colourful shading representing consumer and producer surpluses and deadweight loss, are inadequate to reconcile these two competing ideals of property. One must turn to moral philosophy for an answer.

Among the four classical virtues was justice, roughly understood as meaning the virtue of granting to each person what they are due (Pieper, 1966). Another way of saying this could be that it is the virtue of giving everyone what they have a right to. This brief chapter will consider what various traditions have suggested about whether human persons have a right to private property, and therefore whether or not justice means taxing them more heavily or taxing them more lightly.

The Divine Gift

An understanding of property rights that is common in "pre-modern" cultures is that owners of the land have a right to it because God, or at least some form of a sovereign supernatural ruler, granted it to them. Many Indigenous peoples on Turtle Island, known to moderns as North America, maintained traditions in which the Great Spirit had given them the land, though perhaps we would recognize this as more of a communal ownership or common property of the people (Eckert, 1993)

Something that more closely resembles what we consider private property would be the arrangement described in the Hebrew Scriptures, or "the Old Testament." There, God tells His chosen people of Israel that He has given them the "promised land" of Canaan. Once the Israelites had claimed this land, the Torah reports, a careful census was taken, and God ordered Moses that the property was to be divided up among different tribes and families, with larger groups receiving larger tracts of property (Numbers 26:51-56). These properties were to be an eternal sacred trust to the families that lived on them, which is why, every seven years, any property that had been sold had to be returned to its original owner as a part of the jubilee celebration (Leviticus 25:13). This was why it was seen as so sacrilegious when a corrupt ruler used deceptive and violent means to kill Naboth and take his vineyard, Naboth having refused to sell "the inheritance of my ancestors" (1 Kings 21).

In these texts, God can give the gift of land because, as the creator of the earth, He owns all the land on it (Exodus 9:29; Deuteronomy 10:14; Psalm 24:1; Psalm 50:10-12). This seems to have had implications for Israel's tax policy. There was no property tax to speak of. However, there was what we might recognize as an income tax in the form of a tithe, in which 10%

of everything produced had to be offered to God. In other words, God made and owned the land and allowed the Hebrews to live on it; what the Hebrews made by their efforts was what could be taxed. In modern parlance, we could perhaps call this a tax on production, not on capital (Rushdoony, 1973).

The Stagirite's Insight

If Western culture is, in some sense, a combination of Jerusalem and Athens (connected through the aqueducts of Rome), and we have already looked toward Jerusalem, we should also take a moment to look at Athens, as represented by its two brightest luminaries, Plato and Aristotle.

In book five of the Republic, Plato depicts his mentor Socrates postulating that the guardians of his ideal city would completely relinquish ownership of private property. This was because, to his thinking, private property necessarily made one focus more on their affairs than on the common good. If you own your property that no one else owns, not only will you value it over the rest of the city, but your success will necessarily be someone else's misfortune (if you own something, someone else lacks it). Instead, there should be common ownership of all goods, at least among the rulers of the city, who are meant to be its "best and brightest." This kind of communism will make everyone fully invested in the good of the entire community. (Notice that the Republic advocates essentially abolishing the family unit for the same reason: If only a few people are your brothers, they will be more dear to you than the rest of the population, but, if everyone in the city is your brother, you will love all your fellow citizens equally and be perfectly civic-minded.)

Plato's student, Aristotle, took a different view of this question. To understand Aristotle's view regarding property, it is necessary to understand his ethics. For Aristotle, happiness consists of enjoying the goods that complete our human nature. These include material goods such as a certain level of health and wealth, but, because humans are rational animals and not mere brutes, it also involves higher goods, such as friendship and intellectual activity. In short, happiness means living well, which includes being virtuous, as he explains in his Nicomachean Ethics.

This has implications for his views on property. In his book entitled Politics, Aristotle explains that contra Plato, private property is not a cause of selfishness, but is necessary to cure selfishness. "There is the greatest pleasure in doing a kindness or service to friends or guests or companions," Aristotle observes, "which can only be rendered when a man has private property." On the other hand, if property is held in common, "no one will be known to be generous or do generous actions since the work of generosity is in the use of one's possessions." If being good means being virtuous and being virtuous includes being generous, you need to own property with which you can be generous to others. Pure communal ownership removes the possibility of this virtue.

But isn't that worth it if it means everyone has access to goods and no one needs to fight for what they need anymore? Aristotle rejects this premise. Contrary to those who say that private property is the cause of conflict, Aristotle asserts that "it is a fact of common observation that those who own common property, and share in its management, are far more at variance with one another than those who have property separately." Perhaps my readers who have ever been forced to "share" their toys, or do group work on an assignment, will have some insight into what Aristotle is suggesting here. On the other hand, [W]hen everyone has a distinct interest, men will not complain of one another, and they will make more progress because everyone will be attending to his own business."

How, then, can the problems of poverty be remedied? Remember again that, for Aristotle, the good life requires friendship. For him, this is the solution, not the abolition of private property. "I do not think that property ought to be common, as some maintain, but only that by friendly consent there should be a common use of it; and that no citizen should be in want of subsistence." Aristotle may well have supported the existence of fraternal organizations like the Knights of Columbus, which provide a space for socialization and friendship among men while also providing financial support to their members by way of a common voluntary fund and insurance or retirement plan.

Aristotle thus offers a philosophical basis for saying that the virtue of justice requires the institution of private property, though it is worth remembering that he excluded women and slaves from this realm (Miller, 2022).

What Christianity Brought

With Christianity comes a new view of reality in which God Himself has taken the form of a human being Who described Himself as homeless (Matthew 8:20) and Who commanded His followers to give their extra clothing to the poor (Luke 3:11) and rich men to sell everything they had and give the proceeds to the poor (Matthew 19:21). In this dramatic new preaching, a theme from the Old Testament is developed: God created the earth and gave it to the whole human race. Thus, if there is someone poor who lacks what they need, and you happen to have more than you need, that excess belongs to the poor and you are robbing it from them. Indeed, if that poor person dies, their blood is in some sense on your hands. This is given even more weight by Jesus' pronouncement that, in some sense, He is to be found in the poor (Matthew 25:40).

This is taken quite seriously by the church fathers. As St. Ambrose puts it, "You are not making a gift of what is yours to the poor man, but you are giving him back what is his. You have been appropriating things that are meant to be for the common use of everyone. The earth belongs to everyone, not to the rich." St. Basil the Great (2009) similarly declares in a sermon, "The bread in your cupboard belongs to the hungry man; the coat hanging in your closet belongs to the man who needs it; the shoes rotting in your closet belong to the man who has no shoes; the money which you put into the bank belongs to the poor. You do wrong to everyone you could help but fail to help."

Fuelling these moral injunctions was a particular understanding of the opening chapters of the Bible. A common interpretation of Genesis 1-4, dating back to at least St. Augustine, held that, when God created Adam and put him in the Garden of Eden, there was no such thing as property at that point, and that private property was only instituted after Adam's fall brought sin and violence into the world. (Augustine similarly saw human government as a postlapsarian innovation, which would have been unnecessary if humans had never sinned.)

This was challenged in the fourteenth century with the existence of the Franciscans. St. Francis of Assisi had famously renounced all his possessions and founded an order of friars with a similar dedication to poverty. As time went on and the order became more established, questions arose about how the Franciscans could, for example, have their buildings in which to live (friaries). Some friars, like St. Bonaventure, developed explanations of how this was possible.

The basic form these arguments took was that absolute poverty was a return to humanity's original state of innocence in Paradise. It was also an imitation of Jesus Christ, the new Adam Who also lived in perfect poverty. The Franciscans did not own any property; they simply used property. The Pope was the true owner of their goods. All they were doing was using it for their ministry.

This led to a series of debates within the Church over topics such as whether human law could be transcended by a return to a paradisiacal state (Frank, 2008), whether Jesus did live in absolute poverty or whether He owned a purse, and whether or not Adam owned private property before he ate the forbidden fruit. In asserting in his bull Quia Vir Reprobus that Adam did own property in Eden, Pope John XXII seemed to endorse the view that private property is a part of human nature, not just a historical concession to human sinfulness (Oakley, 1986).

Subsequently, Catholic Social Teaching would continue to maintain that private property is, in some real sense, "sacred." This is because human beings have not only the right but in many cases the duty to protect and support themselves, and this is only possible if they have property of their own. However, private ownership does not negate public use. There is a universal destination of goods; God created the world for everyone to enjoy. Thus, there is a social mortgage on property, meaning you are to use your property for the service and help of others. If you have more goods than you need, and you withhold those excess goods from the poor, then, in those particular cases, they may have the right to take it from you without your consent. This is not stealing, because it properly belongs to them. (The possible implications of this for tax policy are obvious.) Finally, the preferential option for the poor states that, because Jesus is somehow present in the marginalized and disenfranchised, a society is judged by how it treats "the least of these," not by how seemingly successful its economy is.

John Locke: Medievalist or Modern?

Through their reliance on religious authorities, these moral theories of property may be considered pre-modern or irrelevant by some. If we want a justification of property rights for today, it would need to be purely rational and not rely on any theological assumptions. For this reason, John Locke is considered the authoritative writer on the modern defense of property rights, since his labour theory of property seems to rest on secular (and thus supposedly rational) foundations.

But Locke is also a theologian. His First Treatise on Government is a debate over the meaning of the Book of Genesis with Robert Filmer, who read it in a way that justified an absolute monarchy, and his account of private property in his Second Treatise is also based on an exposition of the Genesis story of the creation of Adam. Chapter five, which contains his celebrated discussion of poverty, opens by quoting Scripture to establish that "God...has given the earth to the children of men; given it to mankind in common." He thus situates his argument firmly within the Christian and medieval tradition (Swanson, 1997).

How, then, can any part of the world, which is owned by the entire human race, become a person's private property? Locke begins his explanation by asserting that human beings own their bodies as property. He does not explain or defend this, perhaps assuming it to be obvious or axiomatic. Hans-Hermann Hoppe (2017) has attempted to prove that the very process of engaging in a debate presupposes the idea that the partners in a debate each have ownership over their bodies; the fact that I try to persuade someone to do a certain thing with their body rather than force them to do what I think they should is a tacit concession that they have property rights over their body that I do not have.

Having posited that each person owns their own body, Locke further reasons that "[t]he labour of his body, and the work of his hands is his." Thus, "Whatsoever then he removes out of the state that nature hath provided, and left it in, he hath mixed his labour with, and joined to it something that is his own, and thereby makes it his property." When a person nourishes themselves by eating apples, Locke reasons, those apples did not become theirs when they put them in their mouth; they became theirs when they plucked the apple off the tree. That application of labour was a form of mixing one's body with a part of nature and thus appropriating what was once common property to become private property.

The libertarian thinker Robert Nozick critiqued this by asking exactly what constituted mixing something with one's labour. If I pour a can of tomato juice into the ocean, isn't that a form of mixing nature with my labour? Does that mean the whole ocean is mine, or does it simply mean I've wasted some tomato juice? (Nozick, 1974).

But it is worth recognizing exactly what Locke understands by this mixing. As he puts it, "God gave the world to men in common; but since he gave it to them for their benefit, and the greatest conveniences of life they were capable to draw from it, it cannot be supposed he meant it should always remain common and uncultivated. He gave it to the use of the industrious and rational, (and labour was to be his title to it;)..." The point is not that someone could, say, urinate on a tract of land and thus claim they had mixed it with their body and made it theirs. The point is that, for the earth to be enjoyed the way God intended for it to be, it needs to be cultivated into a useful form. Labour that productively reshapes a part of nature into a form where it serves, nourishes or supports the one who exerted that labour is what makes it that person's private property. In a sense, to continue using Biblical language, we could say that this kind of labour makes that part of the world into the labourer's image.

It has been objected that Locke's reasoning here justifies the displacement of Indigenous people from their land, since they did not tend to have agriculture, which Locke seems to see as defining the kind of labour that turns land into property. But it is worth noting that Locke sees the "Indian" as already exercising the kind of property-generating labour he is describing. "The fruit, or venison, which nourishes the wild Indian, who knows no enclosure, and is still a tenant in common, must be his, and so his, i.e. a part of him, that another can no longer have any right to it before it can do him any good for the support of his life...Thus this law of reason makes the deer that Indian's who hath killed it; it is allowed to be his goods, who hath bestowed his labour upon it, though before it was the common right of everyone." Would Locke limit this to the fruit or deer that the Indigenous person happens to have personally collected or killed, or would this extend to the entire land upon which they live? This is another critique of Locke: The boundaries of what can become your property once you have started mixing your labour are not necessarily clear.

But it is worth noting that Locke famously adds this proviso to his discussion of property:

"It will perhaps be objected to this, that if gathering the acorns, or other fruits of the earth, &c. makes a right to them, then anyone may engross as much as he will. To which I answer, not so. The same law of nature, that does by this means give us property, does also bound that property too. God has given us all things richly [as] the voice of reason confirmed by inspiration. But how far has he given it to us? To enjoy. As much as anyone can make use of to any advantage of life before it spoils, so much he may by his labour fix a property in whatever is beyond this, is more than his share, and belongs to others" (Locke, 1659, 212).

In other words, one should only accumulate property "at least where there is enough and as good, left in common for others." You cannot go on acquiring property indefinitely, no matter how much you mix your labour; you must leave something for others, or, if you do take something from others, ensure that they are adequately taken care of.

This principle was adopted by the Georgists, who saw ownership of land as unjustifiable since no one ever produced the land itself by their labour, and thus argued that all property should be taxed to provide a basic income for everyone in the community. Notably, the founder of this movement, Henry George, saw this principle enshrined in the medieval feudal system:

"Feudalism recognized — in theory at least — that land belongs to society at large, not to the individual. A fief (a feudal estate) was essentially a trust to which certain obligations were attached. The sovereign was, theoretically, the representative of the collective power and rights of the whole people. Although land was granted to individuals for personal possession, specific duties were required. Through these, some equivalent to the benefits received from the common right was rendered back to the Commonwealth" (George, 1879, 375).

It should be added that the sovereign only had this right because he was seen as being in some sense a representative of God, who was the true owner of the land (Kantorowicz, 1946).

Conclusion

Private property and common ownership of the earth might superficially seem to be in contrast with each other, and certainly, some theorists of property, such as Ayn Rand, would absolutize it to the point where a property owner has no social obligations whatsoever. However, as we have seen, the major tradition of private property rights sees property as being morally grounded in the fact that it is entrusted to property owners by God for stewardship and care for others. Common ownership justifies private property and private property is what makes common ownership, or at least common use, pragmatically effective and tangibly real; people need to own property to preserve themselves, develop it into a useful form, and use it to bless and benefit others. On the other hand, using property against the common good undermines the moral basis underlying the concept of property. From Aristotle down to Locke, and exemplified in the Christian ethic, we see that service to others is both the foundation of and the limit to the idea of morally justified property ownership, and recovery of this balanced medieval understanding may be the philosophical shift we need to build a just future.

References

Carlyle, T. (1849). Occasional discourse on the Negro question. Fraser's Magazine for Town and Country, 40(1), 670-679.

Eckert, A. W. (1993). A sorrow in our heart: The life of Tecumseh. Random House Publishing Group.

Frank, T. (2008). Exploring the boundaries of law in the Middle Ages: Franciscan debates on poverty, property, and inheritance, Law & Literature 20(2), 243-260. doi: 10.1525/lal.2008.20.2.243

George, H. (1879). Progress and poverty. D. Appleton and Company.

Hoppe, H. H. (2017). A primer on Hoppe's argumentation ethics. Mises Institute. Retrieved from https://mises.org/wire/primer-hoppes-argumentation-ethics

Kantorowicz, K. (1946). Laudes regiae: A study in liturgical acclamations and medieval ruler worship. University of California Press.

Locke, J. (1659). Two treatises of government. Whitmore & Fenn.

Miller, F. (2022). Aristotle's political theory. In Stanford Encyclopedia of Philosophy. Stanford University.

Nozick, R. (1974). Anarchy, state, and utopia. Blackwell Publishers Ltd.

Oakley, J. (1986). John XXII and Franciscan innocence. Franciscan Studies, 46(1), 217-226. Retrieved from https://www.jstor.org/stable/41975072

Pieper, J. (1966). The four cardinal virtues: prudence, justice, fortitude, temperance. University of Notre Dame Press.

Proudhon, P. J. (1890). What is property? An inquiry into the principle of right and of government. Humboldt Publishing Company.

Rushdoony, R. J. (1973). The institutes of Biblical law. The Craig Press.

Saint Basil the Great (2009). On Social Justice. SVS Press.

Swanson, S. G. (1997). The medieval foundations of John Locke's theory of property rights: rights of subsistence and the principle of extreme necessity. History of Political Thought 18(3), 399-459. Retrieved from https://www.jstor.org/stable/26217324

Desert Theories of Justice

Stemming from the word "deserves", "deserts" is a moral concept used to evaluate the appropriateness of what one does, should have, or rightly earns as a result of some action or accomplishment. Generally, internal thought processes might suggest that the first person to finish a marathon race deserves first place, a criminal that has been found guilty of a crime deserves some punishment, and the protagonist of a story deserves a happy ending. It is important to note that desert claims involve a particular desert. Feldman and Skow expand on deserts as being "the thing[s] that the deserver is said to deserve." Per Feinberg, familiar deserts include such things as grades, wages, prizes, respect, honors, awards, rights, love, and benefits. Indeed, Leibniz and Kant posit that even happiness should be included among possible deserts. Welfare is also another consideration. These deserts may initially seem to be "positive." However, there are "negative" counterparts. Indeed, some of the items on this list are already negative. For instance, consider the deserts conceptualization of grades. While grades may elicit positive feelings of elation, they may also deleteriously impact students who receive a failing grade for an assignment. Other deserts are uniformly negative: burdens, fines, booby prizes, contempt, dishonors, onerous obligations, penalties, condemnation, hate, etc." (Feldman & Skow, 2015). This chapter examines such cases where individuals' actions may warrant desert benefits given their efforts, productivity, contributions, needs, or merits.

Desert based on effort relies on the effort of the individual and is one of the easiest desert bases to prove because the effort is usually proactive and can be physically observed. However, Cutler notes that "the kind of character that puts forth sustained diligent effort in pursuit of a goal is often manifested within particular circumstances containing the appropriate advantages and opportunities"(Cutler, 2009). I agree with the statement as it provides needed context and does not paint a black-and-white picture of the deserving vs the undeserving. According to Maslow's hierarchy of needs, a person cannot move towards self-actualization (which presents itself in a consistent sustained effort towards a goal) until their physiological needs (food, shelter, clothing), safety needs (physical security, gainful employment), social needs (love, dependable friends, position in the community) and esteem needs (respect, recognition, status) are all met in the order presented. Cutler's statement asserts that an individual that puts forth sustained effort towards self-actualization can do so because they have the rest of their hierarchical needs met. Cutler then asserts:

"that although those lacking opportunities is unfortunate, they can also be considered deserving of opportunity insofar as their society has not delivered the circumstances conducive to equal opportunity (such as inadequate and unsound infrastructure and institutions in dilapidated neighborhoods containing extremely concentrated disadvantage)" (2009).

This divide in resource availability is explicit in capitalist societies where opportunity is regarded as the cornerstone of the economic system. However, one only has to look to see that effort in these societies is not correlated to opportunity. As Cutler explains:

"access to the kinds of advantages discussed above may not be necessary for individuals to exert effort, but this does not undermine the desert of opportunity which the principle seeks to establish. Disadvantaged individuals may indeed exert effort toward the kinds of successes described above. However, the relationship between the differential advantages that the advantaged enjoy and the disproportionate criminality by the least advantaged suggests that legitimate effort-making abilities are linked to sufficient opportunities" (2009).

Desert based on merit or value depends on not only the above-average value an individual possesses but also on how the said value was and continues to be maximized based on preset standards. A soldier that executes a mission outstandingly could have a desert claim, and an athlete that breaks a world record could also have a desert claim. These examples showcase individuals possessing above-average value concerning their peers and exercising said value in an exemplary fashion. As is the fashion in this chapter, we cannot paint a simple binary picture when it comes to the complex concept of deserts. In the case of the soldier, his desert claim is not as straightforward if his mission was found to be immoral even if he was strictly following orders. The athlete that broke the world record could have their desert claim challenged if it is discovered they have a significant natural hormonal advantage over their competitors and the previous world record holder.

Desert can be based on the productivity or contribution of an individual, this desert basis however does not require rigorous sustained effort to be deserving of acknowledgement. The productivity of an individual as mentioned earlier does not necessarily require sustained effort. It does however rely on relativity as the productivity of an individual can only be measured against the standard or set productivity of others. However, economic opportunity has to be examined to provide context for examining productivity as a desert. For example, two recent high school graduates from vastly different backgrounds are hired to work at the same automobile repair shop. Equally as passionate about cars, student A has only had hands-on experience with the old car stationed in his high school's auto class since no one in his immediate family owns a car and they all rely on public transportation, student B has been tinkering with cars all his life as his father's past time hobby is restoring cars and his uncle owns an automobile repair shop. It is only logical to assume student B would be the more productive of the two with considerably less effort on his part and would have a desert claim to the benefits of productivity. Cutler in his thesis gives the example of "a larger, wealthier manufacturer may be able to produce certain goods at a faster and cheaper rate than smaller businesses, thus rendering obsolete the productivity of those on the floor of the smaller manufacturing plants. Those workers in the smaller businesses had a claim to desert-based upon productivity, but now their productivity is incomparable to that of the larger manufacturer who can employ not simply more individuals for less money but can also afford machinery to skip several steps in the process involving manual labour. Nothing has changed with the smaller manufacturer, and yet now he would be considered less deserving on the productivity account." He notes that for desert theorists, it is critical to recognize the limitations of productivity desert claims and how they are affected by societal equality of opportunity (Cutler, 2009).

The meager contributions of an individual to a project or an event might be the reason why the project is successful and cannot be disregarded. For example, detectives investigating a murder may ultimately fail to apprehend the accused but still contribute greatly to the work through crime scene investigations, forensic analyses, interrogations, and paperwork completion. Following this same reasoning, however, a tip from an anonymous caller that successfully brings the investigation to a close has a significant achievement to the completion of the investigation. Accordingly, the anonymous caller would need to be acknowledged as being an important part of the project. But for their contribution, the investigation would have failed.

40

Punishment can also be a basis for deserts. An individual who may be deserving of punishment as a result of a wrongful action cannot be punished unless the individual is found guilty of the wrongful act. Contrary to the desert bases listed earlier, the individuals that fall under this basis are not actively seeking desert retribution. The age-old adage of the thief stealing bread to feed his family, Robin hood, and his stealing from the rich to give to the poor are examples of possible desert claims for punishment that could otherwise be viewed as heroic actions.

The aforementioned desert claims all stem from the actions or inactions of individuals or persons. However, there is no real barrier that limits desert claims to only people, as no persons or inanimate objects may also be deserving of some form of benefit or retribution. For example,

A remarkable work of art is said to be deserving of preservation, a vintage luxury automobile deserves to be restored, and a place or venue where unthinkable immoral acts took place deserves to be torn down.

Also important in evaluating desert claims is also the distributor, Feldman and Skow also outlined the role of the distributor as "the person or institution from whom the deserver deserves to receive the desert. In some cases, the identity of the distributor will be clear. In other cases, it is not so clear. Consider, for example, the motto that McDonald's restaurants formerly used: 'You deserve a break today.' No distributor is explicitly mentioned in the motto. It just says that you deserve a break. Perhaps when McDonald's made this statement, they did not have any particular distributor in mind. Maybe they just thought that you deserve it from someone. The same would be true of the Gates Foundation's former motto which is 'Every person deserves the chance to live a healthy and productive life.' The motto does not mention anyone who has the job of ensuring that everyone gets a chance to live a healthy and productive life. Given that it is untenable to ensure that everyone lives a healthy and productive life, it may be that in this case no distributor is mentioned precisely because no one is qualified to be a distributor" (Feldman & Skow, 2015).

Before examining the theories of justice concerning deserts, it is important to examine other theories of justice briefly to provide a standing understanding of justice theories in general. Justice based on equality is the first perspective under examination. Initially developed by John Rawls, this perspective on justice first requires equal distribution of social values - wealth, income, opportunity, outcome, welfare, self-respect et cetera, and by extension justice among all members of society. Rawls outlines these principles in a two-point lexical order he coined the Difference Principle. The difference principle states that: first, each person has an equal claim to a fully adequate scheme of equal basic rights and liberties, which scheme is compatible with the same scheme for all; and in this scheme the equal political liberties, and only those liberties, are to be guaranteed their fair value and second, social and economic inequalities are to satisfy two conditions, namely: that they are to be attached to positions and offices open to all under conditions of fair equality of opportunity, and; they are to be to the greatest benefit of the least advantaged members of society (Lamont & Favor, 2017). However, the Rawls Principle provides pretty explicit guidance on the kinds of arguments that will be accepted as reasons for inequality. Although Rawls is not inherently opposed to a system of rigid equality, he is concerned about the absolute rather than relative status of the group with the least advantages. The Difference Principle supports strict equality if it increases the absolute position of those with the least privilege in society. The Difference Principle dictates inequality up to the point where the least advantaged person's absolute position can no longer be raised by having certain income and wealth discrepancies. Implementing justice in an essentially egalitarian society would provide outcomes where the parties involved in the litigation would be provided terms of justice that are considered fair to the seeker and defending sides.

The restorative perspective on justice is the approach that encourages open collaboration and seeks to repair damage or harm done by providing the opportunity for the perpetrator to take active responsibility and steps to soothe the damage done to the victim. This form of justice is founded on the ideas of respect, compassion, and inclusivity and the knowledge that crime is an offense against individuals and interpersonal relationships and it gives victims and communities affected by a crime the chance to talk about the reasons for the crime, its circumstances, and its effects, as well as to address their needs concerning it.

The due process perspective on justice was first established by the fourteenth amendment of the constitution of the United States of America ("USA") and has been adopted by most western countries in some form or the other. It guarantees citizens that their rights to life, liberty, and property cannot be taken away by the government without due process of the law. The due process of law involves procedural due process and substantive due process. Britannica highlights that after decades of contentious interpretation by the Supreme Court of the USA, the concept of due process as it applies to procedural laws and substantive laws has changed. A law now satisfies the due process requirement if it can be rationally viewed as advancing the common good and the means used are compatible with the legitimate public interest. A harsher level of court review, known as the compelling interest test, must be passed if the law aims to restrict a basic right, such as the freedom to vote or the right to travel. In general, economic legislation is supported if the state can identify any potential public advantage that might follow from its adoption. The Supreme Court of the USA has exercised significant oversight over the execution of criminal justice in State courts as well as sporadic influence over state civil and administrative proceedings in determining the procedural safeguards that should be required of the States under the Fourteenth Amendment's due process clause. Its rulings have come under heavy fire for both their excessive interference with State court processes and their failure to treat all of the first ten amendments' particular procedural protections as equally relevant to both State and Federal procedures.

After reviewing the definitions and basis of deserts, and the different perspectives/theories of justice, we will now examine the desert theories of justice. There is evidence in the form of writing that dates back to the time of Plato and Aristotle that intrinsically connects justice with deserts. The broad desert theory of justice also known as "universal desertism" is the idea that justice is obtained or served when participating parties get what they deserve. Feldman and Skow state that the "universal desertism" view implies that:

"for there to be perfect justice in a society, every student would have to get every grade that he or she deserves, and every athlete would have to win every competition that he or she deserves to win, every neighbor would have to receive every apology and thank-you note that he or she deserves, and everyone would have to receive the amount of respect, and admiration, and love, and contempt, and good luck that he or she deserves. The society would be a veritable wonderland of requited desert in which no one would have any grounds for complaint about being short-changed about anything" (Feldman & Skow, 2015).

Another form of justice where individuals are allocated what they deserve is the "divine moral justice" a form of desert-based justice that leaves the responsibility to God or a higher power to ensure that people get what they deserve, both on earth and in the afterlife. It can be expanded as the belief that justice is upheld when each person receives from God in the hereafter exactly the level of happiness or misery that he or she deserves based on their level of moral virtue or vice during life. Circumstances may arise where justice is measured at a very high level by universal desertism, whereas it is judged at a very low level by divine moral desertism. This would occur if individuals consistently received the fair dues that they merit on this planet, but in addition, if they never received any heavenly or eternal rewards in a life after death for the virtue or vice that they displayed while they were alive.

Feldman and Skow also highlight another form of desert-based justice which they termed political economic desertism. They explain that "a theory of political economic justice could focus on what we may call "political-economic desert bases." These might include such things as being a citizen; having been unjustifiably harmed by a government agency; having earned a lot of money; being keen on getting into business; being vulnerable to robbers and muggers who might attack. The theory could thus focus on desert bases such that it is the business of a government to take note of the fact that its citizens manifest these bases, and it is the business of that government to try to see to it that its citizens receive the things that they deserve on these bases. They expand on the fact the imagined theory could focus on what is called "political-economic distributors". Where the distributor for an individual is the government of the individual's country or recognized representatives of the said government. The theory could then maintain that there is perfect political-economic distributive justice in the individual's country of residence or citizenship if in every case in which a citizen or resident of that country deserves a political-economic desert in virtue of having a political-economic desert base, the government of his or her country ensures that he or she receives that desert. (Feldman & Skow, 2015).

Seeing as this chapter dives into the concept of deserts, its many forms, basis, and justice perspectives, it is important to note that many others have argued against the notion that deserts are a crucial conceptual element of justice, a reservation that is held by many. Some contend that the idea of a desert is flawed. This is generally known as the metaphysical defense of deserts. Others contend that even if the concept of desert is justifiable, it is impractical to decide what people deserve or to treat them accordingly. The epistemological and pragmatic arguments against desert support these notions. Some contend that desert does not play a significant role in distributive justice, regardless of the strength of the philosophical, epistemological, or pragmatic reasons. Libertarian ideas of justice on both the right and left are examples of this viewpoint.

References

Cutler, M. (n.d.). A compatibilist theory of justice and desert. Scholars. Retrieved from https://scholars.unh.edu/cgi/viewcontent.cgi?article=1117&context=thesis

Encyclopedia Britannica (2019). Cantwell v. Connecticut law case. Britannica. Retrieved from https://www.britannica.com/topic/Cantwell-v-Connecticut

Feldman, F., & Skow, B. (2015). Desert (Stanford Encyclopedia of Philosophy). Stanford Education. Retrieved from https://plato.stanford.edu/entries/desert/#Value

Internet Encyclopedia of Philosophy (n.d.). Desert. Internet Encyclopedia of Philosophy. Retrieved from https://iep.utm.edu/desert/#SH1c

Lamont, J., & Favor, C. (2017). Distributive Justice. In E. N. Zalta (Ed.), Stanford Encyclopedia of Philosophy. Stanford University. Retrieved from https://plato.stanford.edu/entries/justice-distributive/#Scope

Normative Economics as a School of Thought and its Connection to Tax Policy

Taxes and tax policy are often a subject of much controversy in countries and communities around the world. Many people strongly dislike paying taxes and wish that they could keep higher percentages of their salaries and avoid paying so much sales tax to make products cheaper. However, on the other hand, many people are also upset with the quality of services that the government offers, such as healthcare with long wait times, the quality of education, the maintenance of their cities, and more. Tax policy aims to balance these two things, by implementing appropriate rates of taxation, while also providing governments with enough money to offer many essential services. While many readers may be familiar with the concept of taxes, normative economics might be less understood. Before diving into normative economics' connection to tax policy, it is important to have an understanding of the concept of normative economics and what this entails.

Normative economics is based on the principle that economic policies and decisions should be made based on what should happen or what ought to happen, considering the issue or topic under the assumption that society functions in an ideal manner (Kenton, 2020). It includes value judgments that are subjective instead of objective (Higher Rock Education, n.d.). To understand this, consider that everyone has different opinions and moral principles that extend to economics (Higher Rock Education, n.d.). For example, some people think that an acceptable minimum wage is $15 per hour, while others would consider this unethical and believe that the minimum wage should be higher. To elaborate, a statement such as "The minimum wage in Canada should be increased to $17 [per] hour" would be a normative statement as it is based on one's opinion on what an acceptable minimum amount of compensation is for work. It cannot be tested as it is based on the values of individuals and not a cause-and-effect relationship.

A comparable statement that would not be considered normative economics would be "A minimum wage of $17 [per] hour would lead to a lower percentage of adults between the ages of 21 and 25 not being able to afford housing". Since this statement is a statement that can be tested and proved to be true or false, it would not be considered normative economics, as it is not based on a subjective judgment of what ought to be. Another example of a statement that would be considered normative economics would be "there should be no federal taxes for those who make a yearly wage of $50,000 or less". This would be considered normative economics as it is not a statement that can be proven or disproven and is based on the value or moral principle that people below a certain income should not have to pay taxes. To demonstrate, a statement on the same topic that would not be considered normative economics is "If federal taxes are removed for those who make an annual wage below $50,000, taxes would need to be increased by 1% for those who make an annual wage above $150,000 to allow the government to receive the same amount of federal taxes". This statement is based on a principle that could be investigated and proven to be true or false, and it is an objective statement compared to a subjective one. This means that this statement would not be considered to be normative economics.

Now that normative economics has been discussed, it is easy to understand how it could be applied to tax policy. Tax policy is a complex and sometimes controversial area of economics, as there are many different opinions and theories of what ideal tax policies should look like. One question that may arise concerning tax policy is the question of comparing flat-rate taxation to income taxation (Wagner, n.d.). Flat-rate taxation would be a system in which everyone would have to pay the same flat rate of taxation, no matter what their income is (Wagner, n.d.). In comparison, income taxation is a system where the tax rate that people pay is based on what income bracket they are within, with those in higher income brackets paying more taxes than those who are within lower income brackets (Wagner, n.d.). Normative economics would approach this issue from the perspective of people and their human rights (Wagner, n.d.). This means that instead of focusing on how tax policy can support economic growth or modify income distribution, it would need to be considered in terms of how the tax policy can both support and promote the interests of the people who will be impacted by that policy (Wagner, n.d.).

For example, flat-rate taxation will likely involve comparatively lower tax rates for those in higher income brackets and comparatively higher tax rates for those who are in lower income brackets. A normative economic argument may be that "income taxation is superior as those who make less income should not have to contribute the same percentage of taxes as those who have significantly more disposable income". Another normative economic argument related to this subject could be that "flat rate taxation would be a superior system as those who are in a higher income bracket should not be obligated to contribute a higher percentage of their income to taxes as this is unfair." While these statements are directly opposing each other, they are both normative economic arguments as they are based on moral judgements, subjective, and not able to be proven or disproved.

Another important aspect to consider is economic efficiency. Economic efficiency is a concept that describes how well a certain market or firm/organization is performing (Smith, n.d.). Economic efficiency can also be split into many different subcategories, each of which has a different meaning. One type of economic efficiency is production efficiency, which is referring to producing a maximum output at the lowest possible cost of production (Smith, n.d.). An example of production efficiency would be when a company is making winter coats, they would want to minimize the cost of producing a winter coat and maximize the cost at which they sell it. The cost of producing the winter coat would include the cost of materials that the company must buy, the cost of equipment in their facilities, the cost of wages of their employees, and the cost of transportation to facilities where the coat can be sold. To have optimal production efficiency the company would minimize all those costs, and maximize the price at which the coat is sold.

Another type of economic efficiency would be allocative efficiency. Allocative efficiency, as the name implies, includes the allocation of resources between different types of productive activities (Smith, n.d.). For there to be optimal allocative efficiency, resources must be allocated in a way that best satisfies consumer preferences, which will lead to consumers being willing to pay a price that is at least equal to the marginal cost of producing the product (Smith, n.d.). Finally, the last type of economic efficiency that will be discussed is dynamic efficiency. While production and efficiency and allocative efficiency were static types of efficiency, dynamic efficiency would be considered a dynamic measure of efficiency, as indicated by the name (Smith, n.d.). Dynamic efficiency is a measure of economic efficiency that assesses the speed at which companies or firms can adapt to change (Smith, n.d.). This change can include a change in consumer preferences or a change in the technology available that can decrease supply costs (Smith, n.d.).

Dynamic efficiency also includes elements such as the introduction of better work practices and rebranding their company image to better align with the current consumer values (Smith, n.d.). One interesting aspect of dynamic efficiency that is important to keep in mind is that initiatives that will often lower long-run costs may be accompanied by short-term increases in costs, due to the cost of implementation (Smith, n.d.). While these initiatives are still positive in terms of optimizing dynamic efficiency in the long run, they will come with a decrease in production and allocative efficiency upfront (Smith, n.d.).

Now that the concept of economic efficiency and its many subcategories has been discussed, economic efficiency can be considered in terms of normative economics and tax policy. One thing that must be considered when developing tax policy is balancing efficiency with normative ideals (Liscow, n.d.). For example, an efficient policy may be to implement a high tax rate on those who have higher incomes, as they would be able to afford this tax rate and still have a lot of disposable income. After all, one of the principal values behind a substantial amount of tax policies is to redistribute wealth from the rich toward the general population. However, this policy would go against the normative argument that distributing money away from those who earned it is not morally correct. This would be a normative argument, as there is no way to prove or disprove it. However, if we consider an alternative normative argument, which would be that giving the rich more services while taxing them an equal amount as those who have much less is morally wrong, then this policy would align with that normative argument.

For one to decide between these two policies, it would first be necessary to identify one's normative beliefs. Once one is sure about their own normative beliefs, one would be able to think about balancing a policy that aligns with both economic efficiency and one's normative beliefs. For example, if one holds the normative belief that everyone in a society has a right to health care of high quality, education up to the twelfth grade, roads connecting their home to major transportation networks, and childcare, as well as the normative belief that those with a higher income should contribute more to these services as it would be more feasible for them to do so, these normative beliefs will play a large role on the type of tax policies that this individual will believe should be written and implemented. For example, this individual would likely support a tax policy where those with higher incomes contribute a higher percentage of their income to taxes for the government to have sufficient funds to implement programs such as healthcare, education, transportation, and childcare.

On the other hand, if one has identical normative beliefs about the fact that everyone in a society has a right to health care of a specific quality, education up to the twelfth grade, roads connecting their home to major transportation networks, and childcare, but this individual believes that everyone should contribute an equal percentage of their salary to taxes, as they believe that taxing higher salaries at a larger percentage serves as a deterrent for people to work towards higher paying jobs and therefore does not align with their normative beliefs, this individual would likely support a different tax income policy. A tax income policy that this individual may support might consist of every citizen contributing the same percentage of their salary to taxes, as this type of policy would align with their normative beliefs. However, as they are still attempting to support the same amount of services as the first individual in this scenario, this would likely lead to those with lower annual incomes paying a comparatively higher percentage of their income to taxes and those with a higher annual income paying a comparatively lower percentage of their income to taxes.

Now that two similar individuals have been discussed, a third very different case will be presented. This third individual does not believe that taxes should be used to fund services such as healthcare and childcare and instead thinks it should solely be focused on services such as maintaining city infrastructure and national defense and also does not believe that taxes should be based on income at all, as this individual views that as unfair. This person would likely support a tax policy where every individual has to pay a lump sum to the government in taxes each year. This type of tax policy would likely mean that those with lower incomes would find this sum more of a burden compared to those with higher incomes, and it would also likely result in the government's tax budget being lower, as there is a limit to how much money those with a lower income could reasonably be expected to contribute.

Now that we have discussed three policies let us consider each policy's strengths and weaknesses in terms of economic efficiency. Starting with the policy that aligns with the first individual's normative beliefs: a tax policy where those with higher incomes contribute a higher percentage of their income to taxes for the government to have sufficient funds to implement programs such as healthcare, education, transportation, and childcare. This policy would lead to the possibility of this tax program having relatively strong production efficiency. The reason for this is that it will ensure that the tax program is well funded, meaning that there will be enough resources for the tax program to be able to implement high-quality services. It is also likely that this type of tax policy would have strong allocative efficiency, as again there would be enough resources to allocate so that the consumers (those who access the services provided by the taxes) are satisfied.

One aspect of this policy that might lower its allocative efficiency is that those who are contributing a higher percentage of their annual income to taxes (in other words, those with higher incomes in this scenario) may feel more strongly that the allocation of funds to services is not being done correctly if they do not see programs that they believe are beneficial to society or themselves. Finally, this tax policy would also likely have strong dynamic efficiency, as having an ample amount of funds to draw from would allow programs to be created that can withstand unexpected sources of stress (e.g. external threats to the country's well-being, a public health crisis, or a natural disaster). However, one thing that is important to note is that all these measures of efficiency for this tax program depend greatly on how the funds from taxes are managed by the current policy and finance officials. Even if an ideal tax policy is implemented that is fair and ideal for all citizens, if the tax funds are mismanaged after they are collected, this will drastically decrease the production, allocative and dynamic efficiency of the tax program.

With that being said, think of the tax policy that matched the second individual's normative beliefs: a tax income policy that consisted of every citizen contributing the same percentage of their salary to taxes to pay for services such as healthcare, education, transportation, and childcare. Similar to the first tax policy example that was discussed, this policy would likely have reasonably strong productive efficiency, as there would still likely be a fairly large tax budget, as this policy still enables those with higher income to contribute large sums of money towards taxes (as a small percentage of a large income can still result in a large sum). One element that could affect the production efficiency of this system would be that if those with lower incomes are unproportionately burdened by having to pay the same percentage of their salary towards taxes, they may need to use more services such as healthcare and childcare, as they would not be able to afford them otherwise. This could be counterproductive, as this system of tax policy would be resulting in more tax money needing to go towards services such as healthcare to support the now larger need. Another area of efficiency that this policy may not do as well would be allocative efficiency. As those with lower annual incomes may be disproportionately burdened by this policy they may feel like the tax money is not being appropriately allocated, since they might feel like they could personally use that money more efficiently than how policymakers are using it. However, this type of policy would likely have an overall high degree of dynamic efficiency, as there would be sufficient funds for it to be adaptable to changes and stresses that might unexpectedly be placed on society.

Finally, moving on to the tax policy that would support the third hypothetical individual's normative beliefs: a tax policy where every individual had to pay a lump sum to the government in taxes each year but programs such as healthcare and childcare are not covered by tax funds. This program would likely have a high production efficiency, as the tax budget would likely be quite low for this policy. That would force policymakers to not spend money unnecessarily as they would be working within a bare-bones budget. However, this program would likely have varying allocative efficiency depending on whom was asked, as some people will agree with the spending allocations while others will disagree depending on what services people believe should be made available. Finally, this program would likely have low dynamic efficiency as it would be very difficult for a program such as this one to overcome change and unexpected stresses, as it would likely be a very strained system from the beginning.

These three examples demonstrate the importance of considering both normative beliefs and economic efficiency when developing tax policies. They also demonstrate many of the difficulties that can arise when attempting to balance normative beliefs with economic efficiency and the controversy that normative economics can cause, as they are based on normative beliefs, which are individual beliefs that are not shared amongst every individual within a society.

After thoroughly considering the complex topics of normative economics and economic efficiency, it is easy to see how applicable these topics are to the subject of tax policy. However, it is also clear how there are many different ways to apply these topics that indicate different tax policies are superior. One must take the time to thoroughly consider their own normative beliefs, and then balance these in terms of economic efficiency to fully establish an opinion on tax policy.

Considering this, it is likely that tax policy will remain a subject where there are always differing opinions and controversies, but policymakers must altruistically continue to strive towards a solution that will be the most ideal for everyone involved.

References

Kenton, W. (2020). Normative Economics: Definition, Characteristics, and Examples. Investopedia. Retrieved from https://www.investopedia.com/terms/n/normativeeconomics.asp

Higher Rock Education (n.d.). Definition of Normative Economics. Higher Rock Education. Retrieved from https://www.higherrockeducation.org/glossary-of-terms/normative-economics

Wagner, R., Normative And Positive Foundations Of Tax Reform. (n.d.). Cato Journal 5(1), 385-406. Retrieved from https://www.cato.org/sites/cato.org/files/serials/files/cato-journal/1985/11/cj5n2-2.pdf

Smith, R., (n.d.). Economic efficiency—Concurrences. Concurrences. Retrieved from https://www.concurrences.com/en/dictionary/economic-efficiency

Liscow, Z., (n.d.). Is Efficiency Biased? The University of Chicago Law Review. Retrieved from https://lawreview.uchicago.edu/publication/efficiency-biased

Justice & Equality

Introduction to Justice & Equality

Justice and equality are both elusive terms that are fraught with differing subjective interpretations. Equality of opportunity and absolute equality is often difficult to measure objectively and place hard and fast guidelines on, especially when it comes to taxation.

The concept of justice is that we all have inherent worth as human beings and that no one's worth is more or lesser than others. Justice asserts that all people should have equal rights and opportunities. Additionally, justice tends to be entrenched in the legal system in some sort of codified way as law. It could be argued that justice is still quite subjective in the sense that different countries and states are governed by different laws, and therefore different "justices." However, the idea is that this concept of justice attempts to level the playing field and remove discrimination in a variety of ways, from access to healthcare to the creation of safer places to live.

The contemporary concept of justice emerged in the nineteenth century, at a time when social mobility was increasing and the middle class was expanding. Various social justice concerns arise at particular times, and some issues may be more relevant in different parts of the world, societies, cultures, and even between neighborhoods around the same city. They have an impact on people's access to various commodities, services, and opportunities. Social justice concerns are frequently broad and varied.

When it comes to equality difficulties, Canada's first nations people face a high proportion of social issues. Incarceration, poverty, unemployment, suicide, addiction, and health concerns are among them. Due to the current high levels of poverty, many of these issues are based on racism and discrimination. While the government has admitted responsibility for past wrongdoings, the issue still exists.

Why is equality just or not?

It is easy to conflate equality as justice but in a world where these ideals have such subjectively entrenched meanings, equality can seemingly be the default stance for justice. Equality may not be always just but equity can be. That being said, extreme inequality - that is, poverty, is not ideal in any society. Poverty has an impact on the strength and resilience of a community. Poverty increases the likelihood of health problems, difficulties finding and retaining a job, involvement with the criminal justice system, and the need for various social assistance.

In 2018, 3.2 million Canadians, or 8.7% of the population lived in poverty. 1.7 million Canadians or 4.6% of the total population lived in deep poverty—having disposable income below 75% of Canada's Official Poverty Line. (Statistics Canada)

It is notoriously difficult to calculate the social cost of poverty. Our criminal justice, health, and social assistance systems, as well as all levels of government, are affected. There are also financial costs: families without money are unable to purchase goods or services.

What are the points in favour and against?

One of the most vitriol-infused debates is that between vertical equity and individual equity. Vertical equity is often presented as progressive tax and expenditure structures, while individual equity is that which individuals freely engage in transactions of their choosing. What is just at the individual level is not always just at the societal level.

Thinking in terms of simplicity, an arbitrarily applied flat or proportional tax might be easy to administer. A flat tax is a constant fee that would be charged, whereas a proportional tax is a percentage fee. It would offer equality in its purest sense. Every member of the populace would have to pay x amount of money to the governmental institution. However, this simplicity neglects the multivariate analysis of the individual - are these people capable of paying this amount given their socioeconomic status? Is the tax amount too lax or exploitative? Will bordering countries or states offer adequately lower taxes that encourage migration?

In a progressive tax system, inflation can sometimes put the onus too heavily on those in the highest tax brackets. This prevents them from obtaining a proportional income to the quality of the work that they put in. This is often the justification that allows for injustices to be committed under the pretense that the system is not fair. Similarly, in proportional tax systems, there is the opposite concern - one would have to justify and establish a minimum wage or income threshold under which no tax should be paid. With rising prices and costs of living, this continues to become a more and more charged topic with more nuanced and complex views to consider.

Why does inequality matter?

As a social security net, taxes can also provide for welfare programs like employment insurance, healthcare, and education that allow people of lower socioeconomic status and marginalised individuals to access vital services and put them on level ground in society. However, in a capitalist society, there can be other social barriers that prevent upward mobility and maintain income disparity. At an individual level, a financially illiterate person may not be able to manage their finances and end up at a significant disadvantage. Unfortunately, taxation often does not take into account the literacy or other systemic issues that may be at play.

January 2020 presented a world that no one was familiar with, none was prepared for, but everyone had to face it. No matter the magnitude of a warning, humans could not have created an immediate society in place of the one we are so connected to. A world with busy traffic, people travelling here and there, and chatters from every direction all came to an abrupt stop. This created the inertia of a socially based society, wanting to connect and engage with the world around them. The tension is felt through the now empty streets, with the faint sounds of street lighting humming. Society is no longer the same, the tension creates generalised details to address fairness, justice, and equity for students. Students are on their path to integrating with the working society consisting of established rules, laws, and procedures. Society is built on the foundation of different ways of being as described by John Rawl's basis of the political theory of modus vivendi]. Conflict arises when there are differences in interest, belief, value, ideology, culture, identity, faith, or ethnicity (Jones, 2017). When conflicts are not resolved, injustice is often the result. This concept is strongly highlighted in the motion of the coronavirus pandemic. People need the support, tools, and most importantly a justice system to be established to reflect the immediate changes in society.

Higher education is incorporated into the capitalist society of the Western world as an economic market. Policy-making in a democratic government represents the reproduction of dominant ideals. With the documented majority of the population reflecting the same constructs, these ideals become institutionalised. It is important to note the ideas change in response to the changes society experiences. The pandemic created chaos the world is experiencing for the first time in the 21st century. The last global pandemic took place in the 1918 pandemic, with an estimated death of 50 million worldwide (Centers for Disease Control and Prevention, 2018). The 2020 pandemic has emphasised the flaws of a capitalist society. The GDP is expected to fall by 3% to 15% in certain countries as a result of the global lockdown (Fernades, 2020). The stock market is an immediate indicator of the severity of an economic crash as it falls from 30% to 50% (Fernades, 2020). These impacts are further noted by the implied volatility represented by the VIX index, otherwise known as the "fear index", based on the S&P 500 index (Fernades, 2020). This index reflects the uncertainty of the economic society due to the instability of the social environment. The average VIX index averages around 20% as observed from 1991 to 2008. During the 2008 to 2009 economic crisis, this index reflected a reach of 80% (Fernades, 2020). In the 21st-century pandemic, this index has reached 80% and is still climbing as of August 2020 (Fernades, 2020). Due to the unprecedented economic trend, effective policies are difficult to establish in a competitive capitalist society.

The advancement of technology in the 21st century allows higher education to be integrated through online and virtual education. Through cancelation of labs, institutional events, restriction to facilities, and discontinuation of all activities associated with higher education. The quality of education is under question with consideration of tuition. Structural inequalities are projected in times of economic disruption reflected in legal problems reflected in the cost of higher education. Other factors exacerbating economic fallouts include student employment, housing, and educational debts. As institutions facing crises during unprecedented times force innovation. Injustice must be questioned and challenged to deliver justice and incorporate digital transformation. This is a time to reflect on the advancements of technology in the present to restructure the justice system to better the future.

Another economic aspect to consider about modernization, automation, and technology is the rising income inequality among the labour force. This is because new technology will have different impacts on jobs. For high-skilled workers, these new technological systems will have a more productive impact when compared to low-skilled workers. This concept is called Skill-Biased Technological Change (SBTC) and 85% of economists believe that SBTC will be a major cause of inequality in the near future (Aziz, 2020). Therefore, the incomes of the high-skilled workers, who typically have higher education and more experience will increase, while the incomes of the low-skilled workers will remain stagnant. This trend has already been seen with the job markets in the United States of America, which shows that there has been a 70% raise in income for males with Masters' and Doctorate degrees, while the wages of male high school dropouts haven't significantly increased (Aziz, 2020).

On a similar note, if income inequality increases, then it is projected that the average household wealth inequality will increase as well. This is because automation would result in products and services being cheaper, hence the economic gains can then be distributed in three ways. One is that there would be less prices on products due to economies of scale, thus benefiting consumers. Next, it can benefit workers through higher wages, and finally, it can increase the profit margins for the owners of the business. Different businesses would distribute the gains in various orders, which would ultimately result in the inequality of wealth. Additionally, another phenomenon known as "deepening automation," can also contribute to this inequality. Deepening automation is used to describe when a task that is already automated is made even more productive through technology. This has the potential to then displace even more of the labour force, which would result in lower economic benefits for these workers over time.

As socioeconomic inequalities are projected during economic instability, restricting access to resources for maintaining physical and mental health. Many resources were accessible through social institutions from government support programs. Due to the closure of social facilities, these programs can no longer reach their intended audience. As society faces injustice due to the conflict between public health and socioeconomic status (SES), demand for change is projected through worldwide movements to establish social equality and social justice.

Low-income children experience a lack of nutrition due to decreased accessibility to nutritious food options. During the COVID-19 pandemic, low-income students no longer have access to nationally funded programs in schools. Schools and child care institutions work with federal and provincial programs to provide programs for those relying on the federal safety net. A study has reported that programs, which include the U.S. Department of Agriculture (USDA) National School Lunch Program, School Breakfast Program, and Child and Adult Care Food Program, serve nearly 35 million children daily. This allowed for the delivery of nutritional health to the families who needed assistance. These programs allowed students to attain two-thirds of children's recommended nutritional needs. Providing nutritious meals is essential to a child's growth during critical times of development. Without attaining essential nutrients and energy children will become fatigued, with reduced immune systems, increasing the risk of contracting communicable diseases. Long-term effects limit a child's psychological, physical, and emotional health. Since schools are shut down due to the pandemic, it becomes harder to feed vital nutrition to children from low-income families(Dunn et al, 2020). Solutions need to be established to maintain social equity for students' health.

Mental health is another area of individual health that must be addressed during the pandemic. The pandemic has projected another area of social stress that has not been presented before. The present health of a nation influences the long-term impacts of the COVID-19 crisis (Laura, 2020). The present social system is not functional during the restrictions presented during a pandemic. A new, updated, and improved social contract must be established to strengthen the health of the nation (Laura, 2020). Students are heavily influenced by the situations caused by the pandemic (Laura, 2020). Students are no longer allowed to physically interact with one another, increasing strain on a child's development. This pandemic has exposed the unjustness of our social system through the lack of fairness, injustice, and inequities. Those students who are in a lower SES family face limited access to technology. The pandemic forced the world to rely on technology as a form of communication. Without access, students are no longer allowed to engage with the world around them. There has been a concerning rise in deaths due to overdoses, alcohol, and suicides. This is often referred to as such "death of despair" as it reflects the studied relationship between low SES and social wellbeing (Laura, 2020).

The education system is one of the most diverse institutional establishments present in the 21st century. As education continues to form higher education, diversity is projected and reinforced. The pandemic has not ignored social injustice during a time in which people are forced in doors but has led to worldwide movements. The racial gap stems from the education received during the development of children. Education is essential to close the gap of racial inequalities. In the United States, black students have lagged behind white students in graduation rate, acceptance rate, and grade percentile. Education involves a multitude of influential factors determining educational performance. A notable factor is how children are received and treated by education staff, including teachers and administrative staff (Weir, 2016). Disparities need to be addressed to initiate change to inequalities experienced at school.

University of Maryland psychologist Melanie Killen, Ph.D. notes that "everyone holds biases of one kind or another...Maybe we can't eliminate them, but we can do all we can to avoid acting on them" (Weir, 2016). Child development should not be discriminated against, especially in educational institutions. Policies are put in place to limit social injustice, but change needs to stem from a societal body. Change needs to be a global movement, voices need to be heard. Society is composed of a diverse community, it should never be oppressed but empowered.

These unprecedented times have exposed issues surrounding fairness, justice, and equity for people. The pandemic has allowed society to analyze present establishments and challenge ideologies of the past. Society is always changing, it is not stationary, nor should societal regulations. Social change must reflect human interactions to transform social culture and institutions. Changes take place over time, having significant long-term consequences. Social justice needs to be established for the future promoting fair regulations and accessibility of benefits for all individuals and groups constituting a society.

Unfortunately, there can be some rather unfavorable repercussions as a result of this type of income inequality that can be further exacerbated by taxation systems; particularly, the epidemic of tax evasion and avoidance that has reached an unprecedented scale. For example, the International Consortium of Investigative Journalists (ICIJ) leaked several scandalous reports, including the Panama Papers and the Paradise Papers, detailing how tax evasion and avoidance practices have become commonplace internationally. Both large multinational corporations and smaller private companies/individuals have been actively capitalizing on profits by relocating their capital to foreign banks as a way to bypass paying taxes in their home countries. In doing so, stakeholders can create tax havens, a channel of untaxed income that goes unnoticed by regulators and bureaucracy. (Oxfam, 2022)

Conclusion

People without access to running water, refugees, migrants, or displaced persons also suffer disproportionately from the pandemic and its aftermath – whether due to limited movement, fewer employment opportunities, increased xenophobia, etc. Additionally, several social issues such as food security, domestic violence, and social isolation are being exacerbated, and social inequities continue to be highlighted as a result of current stressors. If the government does not initiate new long-term public policies to address the social crisis caused by the pandemic and its aftermath, issues such as inequality, exclusion, discrimination, and global unemployment may be further deepened within these networks of societies. Comprehensive social protection systems that provide basic income security are needed to protect workers, reduce the prevalence of poverty, and enhance people's ability to manage and overcome shocks.

Most of the conflict that has emerged in the history of human civilization is a result of the walls people create between themselves. Doctor Paul Farmer's statement, "the idea that some lives matter less is the root of all that's wrong with the world," reflects one result this division creates, a distorted mentality based on principles of inequality. The divergence this division creates between individuals spark conflict within and between societies. We must operate on some level of equality, at least in terms of the way we value other lives and livelihoods, people's rights and responsibilities, as well as their values and worldviews. Unfortunately, these attitudinal and functional inequalities can result in alternate and often conflicting values of justice.

Regional, provincial, and national governments are responding rapidly with social policies to the economic impacts of COVID-19, climate change, and other crises by establishing individual benefits, wage subsidies, business sector supports, grant programs, tax payment deferral options, and other social policies. These policies strive to mitigate immediate impacts; however, since these supports are time-limited, they could result in increased social issues relating to housing, food security, and mental health when the deferrals or benefits stop.

References

Aziz, I. The Effects of Skill-Biased Technical Change on Income Distributions. York University Retrieved from https://yorkspace.library.yorku.ca/xmlui/bitstream/handle/10315/37931/Aziz_Imran_2020_PhD.pdf?sequence=2&isAllowed=y. Ph.D. dissertation.

Center for Disease Control and Prevention. (2018). History of 1918 Flu Pandemic. Center for Disease Control and Preventon. Retrieved from https://www.cdc.gov/flu/pandemic-resources/1918-commemoration/1918-pandemic-history.htm

Dunn, C. G., Kenney, E., Fleischhacker, S. E., & Bleich, S. N. (2020). Feeding Low-Income Children during the COVID-19 Pandemic. New England Journal of Medicine, 382(18). doi:10.1056/nejmp2005638

Fernandes, N. (2020). Economic Effects of Coronavirus Outbreak (COVID-19) on the World Economy. SSRN Electronic Journal. doi:10.2139/ssrn.3557504

Jones, P. (2017). The Political Theory of Modus Vivendi. Philosophia 45(1), 443–461. doi: 10.1007/s11406-016-9800-1

Laura, C. F. (2022, Nov 21). The Mental Health Implications of COVID-19 on Low-Income Communities and Communities of Color. Federal Reserve Bank of San Francisco. Retrieved from https://www.frbsf.org/community-development/publications/community-development-research-briefs/2020/may/the-mental-health-implications-of-covid-19-on-low-income-communities-and-communities-of-color/

Oxfam (2022, Nov 23). Inequality and poverty: the hidden costs of tax dodging. Oxfam International. Retrieved from https://www.oxfam.org/en/inequality-and-poverty-hidden-costs-tax-dodging

Social Planning Council of Peel (2008). Social Exclusion of Minority Groups: A Conceptual Framework. Social Planning Council of Peel. Retrieved from https://www.spcottawa.on.ca/sites/all/files/pdf/2008/Publications/Social-Exclusion-Conceptual-%20Framework.pdf

Statistics Canada (n.d.). Dimension of Poverty Hub. Statistics Canada. Retrieved from https://www.statcan.gc.ca/eng/topics-start/poverty

Statistics Canada (2016). Ethnic and cultural origins of Canadians: Portrait of a rich heritage. Statistics Canada. Retrieved from https://www12.statcan.gc.ca/census-recensement/2016/as-sa/98-200-x/2016016/98-200-x2016016-eng.cfm

Statistics Canada (n.d.). Police-reported Hate Crime in Canada. Statistics Canada. Retrieved from https://www150.statcan.gc.ca/n1/pub/85-002-x/2020001/article/00003-eng.htm

Weir, K. (2016). Inequality at school. Monitor on Psychology, 47(10). Retrieved from http://www.apa.org/monitor/2016/11/cover-inequality-school

Moral and Economic Theories about Redistributive Justice in Tax and Society

Redistributive Justice

The concept of redistributive justice and its appropriate use in tax and society is highly debated amongst politicians, social scientists, and philosophers alike. Distributive justice concerns itself with the socially moral or just distribution of resources amongst a group of people. The redistributive aspect of distributive justice focuses on how to redistribute collected goods, like taxes, to the population in a fair way.

According to the Stanford Encyclopedia of Philosophy, redistribution can be explained in terms of four factors: the subjects, the baseline, the social mechanism, and the goods (Lamont, 2017). The factor "subjects" refers to individuals or groups whose goods are being redistributed. The baseline is the initial distribution of the goods, which must differ from the final redistribution. The social mechanism is the law or policy which governs the redistribution of goods. And finally, the goods are what is being redistributed – often money or property.

The primary goal of redistributive justice in taxation is to distribute a tax burden more equitably across the population so that one's burden is proportional to their wealth (Maloney, n.d.). This redistribution of wealth is meant to ensure that everyone bears some of the burdens of economic growth, but in a way that is equitable to one's circumstance. For some, this is a popular idea – one that equitably redistributes wealth to close the wealth gap between the top one percent and those living below the poverty line. For others, the idea of the government taking and redistributing their wealth through taxation is considered an infringement of their rights and liberties. Some are in support of redistribution in theory but have specific views on the way this should be achieved.

Despite these competing views, the redistribution of wealth happens all the time, due to changes in "systems of taxation and property rights" (Barry 2018). This can manifest in various forms, for example: increasing the minimum wage, reallocating public funds for health care or education, or restructuring the trade markets. Distributive justice is all around us and is an important part of economics, politics, and daily life.

This chapter will discuss the different moral and economic theories that support and challenge the validity of redistributive justice, and under what circumstances a redistribution of wealth is morally and economically justified.

Moral Theories

Before one can begin dissecting the moral theories of redistributive justice, one must first be able to define justice. Is justice about equality or fairness? Is it about receiving what one deserves, or what one needs? Unsurprisingly, not everyone agrees on a definition of what constitutes justice. That personal definition is informed by a person's upbringing, morals, and life experiences.

There are three broad schools of thought surrounding distributive justice. Firstly, the theory of justice as equality; is the belief that everyone should get an equal share of public goods, regardless of their circumstance. This theory fails to account for the fact that individuals have different wants and needs, and that what might be satisfactory for one person may be insufficient for another.

Secondly, the theory of need-based justice; is the belief that people should receive goods based on need, not equality. Some argue that favouring those in need puts those who are not in need at a disadvantage.

Thirdly, the theory of merit-based justice; is the belief that goods should be distributed based on merit or what a person deserves. This theory rewards hard work but doesn't account for the fact that many factors that affect one's life are out of one's control. For example, being born into poverty or inheriting health conditions.

The following theories fall under one of these three schools of thought.

Justice as fairness

The most popular and debated theory of distributive justice is John Rawls' theory of 'Justice as Fairness' which he presents in A Theory of Justice (1971). In his book, Rawls proposes two principles of justice. First, each person has an equal right to adequate basic rights and liberties (Lamont, 2017). Second, social and economic inequalities are to be: attached to positions available to everyone under the requirement of equal opportunity, and; must give the greatest benefits to the most disadvantaged members of society (Lamont, 2017).

Rawls' theory of fairness centers around two basic constants: that citizens should be free people and equal to one another, and that society should be fair and just (Wenar,

2021). The social order of egalitarian liberalism is defined by equality-based reciprocity. Further, he postulates that all goods should be distributed equally, unless "an unequal distribution would be to everyone's advantage" (Wenar, 2021). Essentially, this theory works to make sure that everyone can fulfill their basic needs, and allows inequality so long as the inequality works to level the playing field of society.

Rawls argued that his theory – formally called egalitarian liberalism – was superior to utilitarianism, as it accounted for all the natural inequalities that exist in society. However, some argue this theory is unfair to the upper class who have attained wealth either through hard work or lucky circumstances.

Libertarianism

The most prominent right-wing libertarian in recent history is Robert Nozick (1938-2002), an American philosopher and professor at Harvard University. Nozick is best known for his book Anarchy, State, and Utopia (1974) which provides a libertarian argument to contradict John Rawls' A Theory of Justice.

His three principles of justice state that a person is only entitled to something according to the principle of justice in acquisition, the principle of justice in transfer, or the principle of rectification. In essence, Nozick did not believe that the unequal playing field of life could be evened out, nor that one should try. He accepted inequality and believed that everyone was entitled to the things they owned, so long as they obtained them legally and justly.

This view falls under the political philosophy of libertarianism, which holds personal freedom as its core governing value. Libertarianism has several existing branches, distinguishable by the extent to which they accept authority or state power.

Libertarianism originally evolved out of left-wing politics, particularly the libertarian Marxists and socialists. This left-wing branch was popular in Europe, particularly in the Soviet Union, and called for the fair and equal distribution of all material goods – a concept most colloquially known as communism.

However, the version of libertarianism which dominates North America is right-wing libertarianism and takes a much different stand on the redistribution of wealth. This iteration began in the middle of the 20th century and is characterized by strong rights surrounding private property, individualism, and free market capitalism. In general, right-wing libertarians posit that taxation based on income violates the rights of an individual.

According to The Libertarian Party of Canada, libertarians believe that forcing people to give money to the government through taxation is neither "just nor generous" (n.d.). In their view, the government should be funded by means other than taxation, and welfare or social programs should be provided through voluntary charity. Moreover, a "just" society gives its citizens maximal freedom to do as they like.

Through the lens of a libertarian, redistributive justice is unfair, as it takes goods from an individual to give to someone who has not acquired or traded for it, nor who deserves it due to rectification.

Prioritarianism

Prioritarianism is an ethical and political view that available social welfare should prioritize those who most need it at the moment (Nielsen, 2022). Coined by the ethical philosopher Larry Temkin, this view is similar to utilitarianism, however, it does not weigh the needs of all people equally, but prioritizes those that are in the greatest need. This form of distributive justice is most evident in health care systems, particularly in emergency rooms or organ transplant lists, where those who are in the worst condition are bumped to the top of the waiting list to receive the care they require first.

Viewing redistributive justice through the lens of prioritarianism, a prioritarian would agree with the redistribution of wealth as long as those who are worst off are prioritized or benefit.

Utilitarianism

Utilitarianism can be traced back to the 18th century and the British philosophers Jeremy Bentham and John Stuart Mill who lived from 1747 to 1832 and 1806 to 1873, respectively (Knight, 2014). The theory of utilitarianism focuses on the outcome of an action and does not concern itself with how or why an outcome comes to be. Utilitarianism postulates that an action is good if it causes an increase in the overall welfare of society, and bad if it causes a decrease in overall welfare. Thus the "right" action is that which benefits the greatest number of people in a society.

When viewed through the lens of utilitarianism, redistributive justice is the 'right' action, as it maximizes the welfare of society as a whole (Knight, 2014). However, both historical and modern utilitarians have disputed what constitutes "welfare". Utilitarians tend to replace 'welfare' with "utility", defining utility as "pleasure, happiness, or preference-satisfaction" (Lamont, 2017). This view has its limitations, as it doesn't account for emotion, or what some call "commonsense morality".

For example, the idea of preference satisfaction makes sense on an individual level. A person might decide to sacrifice in some way for some time, such that their quality of life increases in the long run. However, when this example is extrapolated to a larger population, it can be seen as immoral. For example, is it moral to force a large population to sacrifice something if the 'reward' of the suffering will be felt by a different subset of the population? In some ways, this is what happened during the COVID-19 pandemic. The population was forced to quarantine or socially distance themselves for the sake of the most vulnerable in the community. While some were opposed to this idea, the relatively harmless act of wearing a mask and maintaining social distance was generally considered a small price to pay for saving lives. However, utilitarians might disagree with this position as is, or might have disagreed if the cost was higher and the reward lower.

Luck egalitarianism

Luck egalitarianism evolved out of the earlier theory of 'equality of resources" proposed by American philosopher Ronald Dworkin. Dworkin proposed a theory in which people begin on equal footing and with equal resources, but are "allowed to end up with unequal economic benefits as a result of their own choices" (Lamont, 2017). Luck egalitarianism thus asserts that how distribution is undertaken influences justifiability. In other words, the how matters. It proposes a version of distributive justice that aims to "compensate people for undeserved bad luck" (Ekmekçi, 2015). This "bad luck" can come in many forms, among them: illness, accidents, being born into poverty, a difficult family history, etc. However, if an individual is struggling due to their fault – lung cancer due to smoking, poverty due to gambling, unemployment due to laziness – then society has no duty to come to their aid.

While some aspects of luck egalitarianism are positive, it has been harshly criticized for being discriminatory, "incompatible with human dignity, and is in dissonance with real life" (Ekmekçi, 2015).

Conclusions on Morality

There is no one school of thought that triumphs over another, nor is there an empirically 'right' answer to whether or not distributive justice is morally correct. One's personal feelings about the morality of distributive justice and taxation will likely be informed by which school of thought most accurately aligns with their own opinion of what constitutes 'justice'.

When discussing the morality of redistribution, one must determine whether the action of taking and redistributing goods returns something to someone's rightful possession. For example, merely possessing an object does not preclude someone from taking that object away and being morally in the right. If the object came into one's possession through theft, for example then any future repossession or redistribution of the object could restore its rightful possession and thus be morally just. Therefore the "initial possession of goods raises questions about subsequent transfers only if the initial possession is rightful rather than merely physical" (Lamont, 2017). For example, the theft of Indigenous lands in Canada by European colonizers resulted in Europeans physically possessing land but not rightfully possessing it. Thus, an argument can be made that the redistribution of land – or where such a policy is impractical, reparations in other forms – is the morally just choice.

Further, it is important to take into account that wealth inequality in Canada is an issue as closely related to racism as it is to colonialism. In 2016, 20.8% of BIPOC ("Black, Indigenous, and People of Colour") Canadians were considered low-income households, compared to 12.2% of Caucasian citizens (OCASI, n.d.). Further, immigrants were more likely to experience food insecurity and Indigenous individuals were more than twice as likely to experience homelessness than non-Indigenous people (OCASI, n.d.). As a multicultural and multiethnic country, equality has become integral to Canada's identity.

The Canadian Charter of Rights and Freedoms proclaims that "all Canadians have the right to equality, equal opportunity, fair treatment, and an environment free of discrimination based on sex, sexual orientation, marital status, and family status" (Government of Canada, 2019). This right to equal opportunity and fair treatment is what distributive justice works to uphold. In the case of BIPOC people, it is of even greater importance that they receive the aid they need to overcome the institutional racism that continues to persist in our society.

Economic Theories

Taxation is an effective government tool for redistributing wealth and income amongst the population. Regardless of moral disagreements, taxation has many benefits to society and the economy.

The taxes taken from federal, provincial, income, and property taxes are used to finance public services. They fund the development and maintenance of essential infrastructures like roads, schools, and government buildings. They ensure that free public education and health care continue to be a reality for Canada's 38 million people. These social services promote strong and healthy communities, with longer lifespans, greater rates of higher education and literacy, and more skilled workers. Not only is this ideal for social welfare and human happiness, but healthy communities are directly linked to economic growth. Healthy workers take fewer sick days, are more productive, and are more likely to continue to seek higher education and promotion (Healthy Communities, 2017). Taxes also fund emergency services, libraries, waste management, and other public services that everyone benefits from.

In terms of direct redistribution of funds, the taxes Canadians pay contribute towards Employment Insurance, the Canadian Pension Plan, and the Canadian Disability Benefit. These programs directly support those in financial need, those who are seeking work, or those who are no longer able to work due to age, injury, or disability. In this way, Canada's moral theory closely resembles a hybrid of Rawl's vision of 'justice as fairness and the theory of prioritarianism. While it is true that some people will benefit more from social services than others, these programs help to righten inequalities and act as a safety net for all people who find themselves in need.

Canada's taxation system is a progressive one, meaning taxation rates are generally proportional to income (Wong, 2022). Therefore higher-earning citizens are taxed in a higher bracket than minimum wage earners. Canada is not the only country to employ this system. Many countries use some form of progressive taxation, including China, Japan, Australia, New Zealand, the United Kingdom, and most of the European Union. Those with the highest personal income tax rates were Denmark, France, and Austria – with the highest earners taxed up to 55.9%, 55.4%, and 55% of their income respectively (Bunn, 2022).

A progressive system is generally considered the fairest system, however, tax breaks for high-income earners and corporations – in the form of RRSP contributions, charitable donations, etc – undermines the ability of the system to truly distribute wealth effectively and fairly. Distributive justice, in the way that it is currently enforced in Canada through progressive taxation, is meant to ensure a level of fairness in the way goods and income are distributed amongst the population. However, the existence of multi-millionaires and billionaires alongside the 3.98 million Canadians who were living below the poverty line in 2018 is proof that there is great room for improvement (Government of Canada, 2021). In fact, as of October 2022, 80% of polled Canadians believed that the rich should be taxed more than they currently are (Ipsos, 2022).

Conclusion

There exist many different moral theories that both support and contradict the fairness of distributive justice. While the morality of taxation is debatable, its economic benefits are undeniable. The economy thrives when citizens are happy, healthy, and educated.

While some argue that distributive justice infringes on their freedoms, others argue that distributive justice fulfills the social obligations we have to one another, and upholds basic human rights.

Everyone has a right to a different opinion on issues of justice, but the COVID-19 pandemic has highlighted the importance of systems that work to benefit society as a whole, but prioritise the needs of the most vulnerable or at risk. In the past few years, the government has prioritised health and safety through policies meant to limit the spread of disease and funding to prevent those most affected by job losses from losing their homes and livelihoods.

While these policies have not always been preferred or acceptable to all people, as evidenced by protests across the country, they succeeded in their goal to control the pandemic. Redistributive justice funded programs like the Canada Emergency Response Benefit ("CERB") and the Canada Emergency Student Benefit ("CESB") which provided grants to those who were unable to find work during the pandemic. Other social programs, like the Canada Emergency Business Account ("CEBA"), worked to support small businesses to afford rent and operating costs, and restart the economy when social restrictions eventually loosened. Without a system of taxation and collective funding of social programs, the disparities between the wealthy and the poor would have been exacerbated by this unprecedented pandemic. Instead, the pandemic has highlighted how one's fortunes and future can change overnight – by circumstances entirely outside their control – and the importance of having a safety net of social services to cushion the fall and help one back onto their feet.

Thus, in this author's opinion, taxation and distributive justice is a necessary tool for the redistribution of wealth and is morally acceptable for the benefits it affords to the most disadvantaged members of society.

References

Barry, C. (2018). Redistribution. In E. N. Zalta (Ed.), The Stanford Encyclopedia of Philosophy (2018). Metaphysics Research Lab, Stanford University. Retrieved from https://plato.stanford.edu/archives/spr2018/entries/redistribution/

Bunn, D. (2022). Top Personal Income Tax Rates in Europe. Tax Foundation. Retrieved from https://taxfoundation.org/top-personal-income-tax-rates-europe-2022/

Ekmekçi, P. E., & Arda, B. (2015). Luck Egalitarianism, Individual Responsibility and Health. Balkan Medical Journal, 32(3), 244–254. doi: 10.5152/balkanmedj.2015.150012

Government of Canada. (2019). Federal gender equality laws in Canada. GAC. Retrieved from https://www.international.gc.ca/trade-commerce/gender_equality-egalite_genres/lois_can_gen_eq_laws.aspx?lang=eng

Government of Canada. (2021). Building Understanding: The First Report of the National Advisory Council on Poverty [ATI annual report]. Government of Canada. Retrieved from https://www.canada.ca/en/employment-social-development/programs/poverty-reduction/national-advisory-council/reports/2020-annual.html

Healthy communities mean a better economy. (2017). Blue Cross Blue Shield Association. Retrieved from https://www.bcbs.com/the-health-of-america/articles/healthy-communities-mean-better-economy

Ipsos. (2022). More than seven in ten Canadians (72%) believe that the tax burden of individuals is too high; meanwhile, eight in ten (80%) think that the rich should be taxed more. Ipsos. Retrieved from https://www.ipsos.com/en-ca/news-polls/fiscal-issues-canada

Knight, C. (2014). Theories of Distributive Justice and Post-Apartheid South Africa. Politikon, 41(1), 23–38. doi: 10.1080/02589346.2014.885669

Lamont, J., & Favor, C. (2017). Distributive Justice. In E. N. Zalta (Ed.), The Stanford Encyclopedia of Philosophy (Winter 2017). Metaphysics Research Lab, Stanford University. https://plato.stanford.edu/archives/win2017/entries/justice-distributive/

Libertarian Party of Canada. (n.d.). Retrieved from https://www.collectionscanada.gc.ca/eppp-archive/100/205/300/libertarian_party/2006-01-03/english/libertarian-party-faq.html

Maloney, M. A. (n.d.). Distributive Justice: That is the Wealth Tax Issue. Ottawa Law Review, 20(3), 601-635. Retrieved from https://rdo-olr.org/wp-content/uploads/2018/02/olr_20.3_maloney.pdf

Nielsen, L. (2022). Pandemic prioritarianism. Journal of Medical Ethics, 48(4), 236–239. doi: 10.1136/medethics-2020-106910

OCASI. (n.d.). New Fact Sheets Show Growing Racial Disparities in Canada. Ontario Council of Agencies Serving Immigrants. Retrieved from https://ocasi.org/new-fact-sheets-show-growing-racial-disparities-canada

Wenar, L. (2021). John Rawls. In E. N. Zalta (Ed.), The Stanford Encyclopedia of Philosophy (Summer 2021). Metaphysics Research Lab, Stanford University. Retrieved from https://plato.stanford.edu/archives/sum2021/entries/rawls/

What is Libertarianism? (By Marilee Haylock). (n.d.). Retrieved from https://www.collectionscanada.gc.ca/eppp-archive/100/205/300/libertarian_party/2006-01-03/english/libertarianism.html

Wong, M. (2022, October 31). How do tax brackets work in Canada? We make it make sense. Toronto Star. Retrieved from https://www.thestar.com/business/2022/10/31/how-do-tax-brackets-work-in-canada-we-make-it-make-sense.html

Tax and Society: How is Tax Deployed as a Public Policy to Change Behaviour and Influence the Society we Live In

Chapter 7: Tax and society: How is tax deployed as a public policy to change behaviour and influence the society we live in - Abdulrahman Aldada

The quality of life for many households has significantly improved due to globalization and technological progress, particularly digitalization and advancements in automation, which have also helped lower poverty rates in many emerging nations. Globalization, modern technology, and flexible work schedules all benefit society and present excellent chances to enhance well-being. A broader selection of higher quality, more affordable consumer items is available to consumers nowadays. Flexible work schedules might give employees a chance to better balance their professional and personal priorities throughout their lives. Businesses also have more options than ever to innovate and advertise their products and services to a worldwide audience. While these adjustments have led to higher earnings and more opportunities, these gains have not been distributed fairly.

Various economies proceed to endure devalued efficient advancement, frequently stagnant wages, and elevated levels of inequality, notwithstanding recent improvements in economic performance. Furthermore, technological advancements may cause a shift in the demand for labor toward occupations that will call for more extensive use of cognitive skills, for which many employees lack the necessary training at the moment (Kutasi & Perger, 2018). This could widen the salary, employment opportunity, and life prospects gaps between people with high, medium, and low skill levels.

Additionally, as nonstandard employment and the "gig economy" grow, established employment practices and social safety nets may be put under pressure. These elements might make the inequity even worse. It is difficult for policymakers to address the issues of poor productivity growth and rising inequality simultaneously. These problems are brought on by the escalating fiscal strains brought on by aging populations and climate change.

The productivity charges of utilizing taxes on labor and capital to achieve domestic equity goals are increased by the mobility of money and, increasingly, of labor in a globalized and quickly evolving society. Traditional social protection systems are put to the test by technological progress as well as predictions for the upcoming years of occupation; as a result, adjustment mechanisms are needed to help people make the shift (Jun, 2021). Tax policy is sometimes said to encourage either efficiency or equity but not both. There are frequent trade-offs between equity and efficiency goals; for example, policies that promote growth may be counterproductive to reducing inequality, and vice versa. Similar to this, tax reduction may support growth and occasionally equity but may undermine the primary goal of the exaction arrangement, meant to increase civic turnover.

Changes have been made to exaction arrangements to accommodate advancement and modern scientific advancement, specifically in light of the evolving nature of the work-force. Increasing the standard of government consumption is also crucial because it offers individuals liable to pay tax the best return on their investment. Still, plenty can be done, even if thorough reform can be challenging, and it is unclear how future events will affect the economy and tax system (Lee, 2021). Additionally, there are trade-offs between addressing various interrelated disparities and other competing policy objectives, necessitating some objective prioritization. Nevertheless, governments have a crucial role to play in promoting social inclusion and change. Managing these trade-offs poses complicated problems for policymakers, and different countries may have other solutions to these problems.

Increases in inequality, mainly where it is already high, damage people's sense of their well-being and may have detrimental effects on economic growth. Increased productivity can slow growth caused by high-income disparity, and individuals with low income and wealth may not have enough opportunity to invest in their abilities. When inequality levels are too high, people may become more doubtful about the benefits of globalization, and political problems may develop in some nations as a result of the sense that the gains from growth are not fairly distributed. Increased social risk and job obsolescence both harm well-being and may put more strain on the government's finances (Lim, 2022). A desire for enhanced communal shielding in reaction to fresh or altering communal threats may put a burden on state budgets in sophisticated countries where economic shocks target specific areas or industries.

Despite the significant expansion of social protection systems in many countries over the past few decades, a sizable portion of the poor in emerging economies continue to be excluded from social safety nets (Smith, 2019). The main problem is to do so in a fiscally viable way. In such nations, rising automation might increase the demand to modify communal protection nets by expanding their reach along with the number of privileges the impoverished citizens get. In industrialized economies, demographic change, particularly population aging and migration, exacerbates these demands on public finances. While making certain that people, particularly young citizens, have acquired technological advancement in addition to employment is a challenging communal monetary burden, population aging is a significant worry in several emerging nations.

Economic structural changes provide difficulties for tax policy in terms of efficiency, equity, and revenue. The resources available to policymakers to address these trends also change, posing new problems for them to solve. In some circumstances, trade-offs between policy options become more complex (Matsumoto, 2021). Numerous elements of tax systems were created with the economy of the past in mind. Thus they might not always be appropriate to foster equitable growth now or in the future. Amendments that are suitable for one nation might not be as crucial in another because each country faces unique tax policies and other issues. To be effective, reform packages must be carefully crafted and implemented in the correct order. Trends posing difficulties for fiscal management and general advancement major inclination Issues with general development issues with exaction regulation minimal expansion in productivity

Real wage growth is slowed by low productivity growth, which also exacerbates business differences and can increase inequality. Productivity stagnation increases the importance of pro-growth tax policy, which might lead to parity 'trade-offs' in a minimum term. If inequality rises, several employees might be passed by expansion, which would be bad for skill investment, health, and well-being (Lim, 2022). Calls necessitate the utilization of exaction arrangements to support efforts to minimize earnings and richness disparity, fostering success, increase as inequality rises, and trade-offs. Also, there may be more significant wage gaps based on skill level and a requirement for lifelong learning as a result of the loss of some existing jobs and the obsolescence of some talents. Increased nonstandard employment may make it easier to reclassify labor as capital income, result in lower SSC revenue, and reduce welfare entitlements, but it may also boost job flexibility.

Overall occupation expansion, although frequently considerable, lacks concentration in few places, thus swift sector switching of jobs. Tax competition increases when companies, capital, and people become more mobile (Hwang, 2022). This may create chances for tax evasion and BEPS behaviors, as well as more significant cross-border spillover impacts of tax policy. The ongoing discussion regarding how tax policy might be utilized to promote economic growth has been triggered by the declining productivity growth in many industrialized countries. The question of how tax policy could simultaneously promote fairness and efficiency goals have been brought up by policymakers who have observed the survival of essential trade-offs linking parity to success in several parts of execution law.

Even if tax policy is frequently the second-best option for promoting general expansion, OECD research on the success of generalness has revealed fresh information on the degree to which the success, as well as fairness goals of the excitation rule, might reinforce one another and promote growth. Exante consideration of both goals in policy design presents a difficulty, for instance, through initiatives that encourage the acquisition of skill and creativity (Hong, 2021).

The burden on tax systems has increased as a result of globalization, digitization, and increasing tax base movement. Nations have worked to lower top Corporate Income Tax and Personal IncomeTax rates over the past few decades because of their adverse effects on the incentives to labor, save, and invest. High-skilled employees may face more tax competition as a result of increased labor mobility, especially for individuals with high skill levels.

Significant discrepancies linking the individual to organization-al execution rates have emerged in several nations as corporate tax rates have decreased, which can encourage individuals to reclassify and incorporate salary income as capital plus corporate earnings. Such reasons have pushed labor income tax rates down, which has led to a decline in tax progressivity during the past few decades, particularly in the highest portion of the income distribution (Nam, 2020). According to recent OECD research, globalization has helped some countries' income taxes have less of a redistributive effect, while personal income taxes' diminishing progressivity, particularly at the top of the distribution, has helped certain nations' total income redistribution.

Policymakers should carefully weigh the advantages and disadvantages of progressivity reductions; While decreased progressivity might lead to an increase in earning disparity during a specific time duration, it might as well enhance inspiration for saving plus investing in people capital, which may lead to rises in lifetime incomes and a decrease in inequality over the long run. A growing number of atypical "gig" jobs and other labor market structural changes complicate tax gathering as well as threaten fairness in addition to the effectiveness of the exaction arrangement (Park & Kim, 2021). In several nations where non-average occupation is a victim of differing proportions under execution and SSC arrangements, the rising prevalence of nonstandard work may present difficulties.

Increased reclassification of labor revenue as business income could result from an increase in nonstandard work. An increase in self-employed people may cause issues with exaction payment turnover collection in different exaction sectors; mainly, third-party levels might drop (Eberharting-er, Speitmann, Sureth-Sloane, & Wu, 2020). Ensuring new nonstandard workers have low compliance burdens will help reduce the risk of their slipping into the informal sector, which is another concern for tax policy. Because of informality, emerging economies will continue to confront difficulties, which will make it more inefficient to establish progressive tax systems. Finally, adjustments to social transfers to account for a rising number of workers in unconventional employment arrangements are challenging due to changes in the labor markets. For tax policymakers, modifications in the international economy bring both chances and threats.

With the use of modern technologies, tax authorities can now battle evasion and BEPS behaviors in more sophisticated ways, notably by more effectively taxing 'gig' and unreported income. The possibility for success, effectiveness, and simplicity of execution collection and computation is further increased by augmented information storage volume and the digitization of transferring funds (Ricci, 2022). The availability of expanded cross-border data to tax authorities will also rise, whether it comes through bank statistics, transaction charging, tax rules, or nationS-by-nation reporting. Social transfers could also be made more effective thanks to advances in information technology, particularly in developing nations. All of these initiatives offer fresh chances for countries to increase revenue in a just and effective way.

The economy's shifting structure also puts additional pressure on consumption. The growth of nonstandard work makes it more difficult to create social protection systems that can cater to these employees' requirements (Deák, 2019). Additionally, the demand from an aging population already puts a strain on social protection spending. There might be increasing tension for bigger expenditure to decrease disparity, invest in schooling and guidance, upgrade outmoded techniques, as well as address fresh and developing kinds of a problem if employment is moved offshore or workers' skills become obsolete.

To transition to more capital-intensive or skill-based production in many developing economies, increased lavish consumption might be necessary for investments in infrastructure, learning as well as research and development ("R&D").

The expenses of income support or other forms of poverty relief for individuals with minimal market earnings and the prices of reducing the detrimental effects of poverty on health and well-being can all be attributed to income inequality (Shin & Suh, 2022). As a result, there is a compelling argument in favor of implementing governmental measures to combat poverty, and lowering market income inequality may be one such policy. Therefore, improving public expenditure quality is crucial to achieving inclusive growth.

Putting a focus on communal investments that might increase success and salary, such as investing to increase educational attainment and upgrade infrastructure, is one way to do this. Public consumption in the form of grants for particular products may exacerbate economic misinterpretations while also being a subpar strategy for reducing income inequality. High-quality public investment can boost tax morale and have a favorable impact on execution income in the segment by boosting reliability in institutions and organizations of governance. To ensure that public finances support inclusive growth, improving the quality of public spending is essential.

According to OECD research, there may be a disparity-effective trade-off depending on the administration's size, with bigger nations being linked to 'lower long-term growth and lower levels of disparity. However, the research indicates that if countries have well-functioning governments, the negative growth effect of large governments can be overcome (De Simone, Stomberg, & Williams, 2018). Regardless of the size of the government, excellent expenditure, regulatory, and policy frameworks can allow for a smaller government sector to nevertheless produce better, more inclusive growth outcomes. Social protection spending is under increased strain due to the quick and ongoing changes in the workplace.

A growing proportion of workers may fall on the outer part of the coverage of the customary social indemnity programs that are accessible to people in a few extra types of hire as a result of shorter job tenure and increased self-employment rates. The viability of social protection systems that rely on SSC funding may be compromised by these exact causes, necessitating increasing financing of SSCs from other sources of income (Blaufus, Lorenz, Milde, Peuthert, & Schwäbe, 2022). These numerous expenditure constraints emphasize how crucial it is to protect the tax system's ability to raise money.

Many middle-income countries today don't generate enough cash to cover their upcoming spending requirements. These include investments that open the door to more significant growth. Investments in school construction and a continued increase in the participation and completion of schooling for kids from lower-income families would aid in enhancing social mobility. Many rising economies also have impoverished infrastructure supply, both in terms of quality and quantity, demonstrating the need for more public investment. Spending on infrastructure in developing economies might as well increase inclusivity and safety by facilitating accessibility to communal transportation, secure power, safe water, plus sanitary facilities (Smith, 2019). Even though the size of the government may differ from one nation to the next, it is still important to raise money in an efficient, equitable, and effective manner to address these issues. Social transfers that reduce inequality must be paid for by sustainable tax income.

According to OECD data, transfers typically have a more significant overall impact on reducing income inequality over time than taxes do. Since the middle of the 1990s, income redistribution in industrialized countries has decreased, primarily due to a decrease in transfer redistribution (Chung & Jung, 2022). Tariffs have had a less significant and more uneven impact on this reduction. The decline in redistribution has resulted in higher levels of disposable income inequality in various nations. In-work benefits might have broader helpful effects on the health of such groupings receiving them and have been found to have a powerful impact in nations with high levels of wage inequality. For rising economies with potentially limited organizational capability, this can be especially troublesome. By utilizing big data, tax administrations may be able to lower these expenditures for both in-work benefits and other conditional cash transfers.

Payroll tax and SSC reductions would benefit workers in several OECD nations, and they might be funded by transferring the cost of communal shielding funding from SSCs to additional execution sectors. Reduced effective tax rates at low incomes can assist businesses that hire a lot of low-skilled labor, which benefits these employees as well. This is in addition to increasing employment. SSC lessening must be taken into account as a section of the larger communal indemnity amendment, as well as operate excellently in conjunction with more extensive structural measures to promote labor market activation, such as incentives for low-skilled workers to invest in their skills (Vlcek, 2018). Many OECD and G20 nations can increase employment by removing political obstacles to women entering the workforce.

Countries should prioritize taking into account the gender impact when designing and monitoring tax and transfer policy measures. Countries may think about reducing the high marginal tax rates imposed on second earners through the modification of tax advantages and allowances for dependent spouses. The majority of current tax breaks and financial incentives for skill investments go to individuals with higher incomes.

Enticements might be directed at low- wages and low-capable groupings to minimize disparity plus promote labor efficiency as low-earning and low-capable employees hold a lesser tendency to participate in skills advancement. However, such targeting can involve trade-offs in terms of both administrative viability and horizontal equity. For skills investments, incentives can include CIT and PIT credits; however, direct spending might also work.

Raising skill levels can boost employment rates and lessen overall tax system distortions. Better skill levels increase the likelihood of higher wages and labor market participation. As a result, committing money to skills might increase labor market engagement as well as lessen the detrimental effects of taxes on employment (Young Seok Park & □□□, 2013). People who are more closely connected to the labor market are less likely to decrease their labor supply in reaction to taxes, which lowers the efficiency losses brought on by income taxes. This could imply that improving skill levels have major economic advantages.

This emphasizes the significance of encouraging skill investments, particularly for people who have a lower attachment to the labor market, such as single parents and both younger and older workers. Innovative approaches, including the provision of financial incentives, are required to assist in training for the low-skilled due to the changing nature of the labor market (BLUM, 2017). The will to encourage the lifelong acquisition of knowledge, especially for individuals with minimal acquaintance, is highlighted by the fact that some people are more in danger than others of having their employment moved offshore or made redundant by technology.

In conclusion, increases in taxation inequality, mainly where it is already high, not only damage people's sense of their well-being but also may have detrimental effects on economic growth. The desire for enhanced communal shielding in reaction to fresh or altering communal threats may put a burden on state budgets in sophisticated countries where economic shocks target specific areas or industries. The main problem is to do so in a fiscally viable way. In such nations, rising automation might increase the demand to modify communal protection nets by expanding their reach along with the number of privileges the impoverished citizens get. Productivity stagnation increases the importance of pro-growth tax policy, which might lead to parity 'trade-offs' in a minimum term. Also, there may be more significant wage gaps based on skill level and a requirement for lifelong learning as a result of the loss of some existing jobs and the obsolescence of some talents.

References

Blaufus, K., Lorenz, D., Milde, M., Peuthert, B., & Schwäbe, A. N. (2022). Negotiating with the tax auditor: Determinants of tax auditors' negotiation strategy choice and the effect on firms' tax adjustments. Accounting, Organizations and Society, 97, 101294. doi: 10.1016/j.aos.2021.101294

Blum, W. J. (2017). Tax Policy in a Democratic Society. National Tax Journal, 2(2), 97–109. doi: 10.1086/ntj41789809

Chung, J. S., & Jung, J. H. (2022). Policy Directions of Capital Gain Tax, Acquisition Tax, and House Rental Income Tax Systems. Korean Society of Tax Law, 7(2), 59–102. doi: 10.37733/tkjt.2022.7.2.59

De Simone, L., Stomberg, B., & Williams, B. (2018). How Tax Enforcement Disparately Affects Domestic Corporations Around the World. SSRN Electronic Journal. doi: 10.2139/ssrn.3225191

Deák, D. (2019). Legal Considerations of Tax Evasion and Tax Avoidance. Society and Economy, 26(1), 41–85. doi: 10.1556/socec.26.2004.1.2

Eberhartinger, E., Speitmann, R., Sureth-Sloane, C., & Wu, Y. (2020). Sweetheart Deals in Tax Bargaining? How Trust Affects Concessionary Behavior. SSRN Electronic Journal. doi: 10.2139/ssrn.3723499

Hong, T. Hwa. (2021). A Study on Improvement Plans for Public Interest Performance and Tax Balance: Focusing on public interest and tax benefits. Korean Society of Tax Law, 6(4), 165–204. doi: 10.37733/tkjt.2021.6.4.167

Hwang, I. G. (2022). Study on the Improvement of Public Trust Taxation System. Korean Society of Tax Law, 7(2), 5–58. doi: 10.37733/tkjt.2022.7.2.5

Jun, D. H. (2021). A Study on the Improvement of Local Tax System on Trust Property. Korean Society of Tax Law, 6(2), 35–73. doi: 10.37733/tkjt.2021.6.2.35

Kutasi, G., & Perger, J. (2018). Tax incentives applied against externalities: International examples of fat tax and carbon tax. Society and Economy, 37(s1), 117–135. doi: 10.1556/204.2015.37.s.8

Lee, D. K. (2021). Study on the effect of digital tax and the global minimum tax on the Korean foreign tax credit system - focusing on preventing international double taxation -. Korean Society of Tax Law, 6(3), 5–40. doi: 10.37733/tkjt.2021.6.3.5

Lim, K. I. (2022). A Study on the Necessity of Introducing Unlisted Stock Valuation. Korean Society of Tax Law, 7(2), 141–170. doi: 10.37733/tkjt.2022.7.2.141

Matsumoto, M. (2021). Tax competition and tax base equalization in the presence of multiple tax instruments. International Tax and Public Finance. doi: 10.1007/s10797-021-09703-z

Nam. (2020). The Structural Commentary on The Current Tax Law. Korean Society of Tax Law, 5(4), 5–40. doi: 10.37733/tkjt.2020.5.4.5

Park, C. D., & Kim, B. I. (2021). Improvement plan for taxation of trust beneficiary rights under the Inheritance Tax and Gift Tax Law. Korean Society of Tax Law, 6(4), 93–135. doi: 10.37733/tkjt.2021.6.4.93

Ricci, M. A. (2022). How better client service performance affects auditors' willingness to challenge management's preferred accounting. Accounting, Organizations and Society, 101377. doi: 10.1016/j.aos.2022.101377

Shin, H. Y., & Suh, H. S. (2022). A study on Securing Effectiveness of the Taxpayer Rights Protection System. Korean Society of Tax Law, 7(2), 103–139. doi: 10.37733/tkjt.2022.7.2.103

Smith, K. W. (2019). The Cultural Grounding of Tax Issues: Insights from Tax Audits. Law & Society Review, 29(3), 437. doi: 10.2307/3053974

Vlcek, W. (2018). The Global Pursuit of Tax Revenue: Would Tax Haven Reform Equal Increased Tax Revenues in Developing States? Global Society, 27(2), 201–216. doi: 10.1080/13600826.2012.762347

Young Seok Park, & □□□. (2013). Tax Attitude, Fair Society Perception, and Tax Behavior. □□□□□□□: □□□□□, 27(3), 109–133. doi: 10.21193/kjspp.2013.27.3.007

Family and Gender-Based Implications of Tax

In this chapter, we will investigate how annual tax forms are impacted by familial relationships and what processes are in place to benefit family units (including both married individuals and common-law partners and their children, if they have any). Later on in the chapter, the unique circumstances of gender-based pricing and taxation will be discussed to conclude this segment on family and gender-based implications of tax to provide further context on this governmental system.

Family Tax Benefits

What relational terms are included in tax forms?

To discuss how tax differs for family units provincially, territorially, and federally, one must first define a legal family unit and how specific terms are used in practice. First, one is considered to be married for tax purposes if they have a spouse and are wedded together (Canada Revenue Agency, n.d.-a). In Canada, marriage and the dissolution of marriage are overseen by both the federal and provincial governments with the provincial government being specifically responsible for creating laws surrounding the ceremonial aspect of marriage or the solemnization of marriage (Canada Revenue Agency, n.d.-b). All provincial territories in Canada have established age requirements, officials who can oversee marriages, witnesses, and the provision of religious or civil ceremonies for marriage. Other strict requirements for a valid and legal marriage include that the spouses must have the capacity to be married which means that the individuals cannot be blood-related and nor can they be related through adoption and the marriage must be monogamous which neither party seeking to marry another person at the time that their original marriage is still valid.

The term common law applies to couples that are not legally married but who live together in a conjugal relationship and either have done so for at least 12 months, have a child together by birth or adoption, or who share child custody (Canada Revenue Agency, n.d.-a). For the 12 months spent living together, the couple cannot be separated for more than 90 days due to a breakdown in the relationship and still be considered to be common-law partners. Common-law relationships differ from marriage in that they are legal de facto relationships where the status is determined for specific cases based on evidence while marriage is a legally de jure relationship that has been established in law (Canada Revenue Agency, n.d.-b).

Other relationship statuses that one may use on their tax forms include "separated" which means that a couple is removed from one another for at least 90 days and applies to both common-law partners and spouses, "widowed" where one's common-law partner or spouse is deceased, "divorced", or "single", as in where no other relational term is applicable (Canada Revenue Agency, n.d.-a). If one is separated from their common-law partner or spouse at the time of filing their tax forms, they must complete a Marriage Status Change form.

How spousal and common-law relationships are impacted by taxation

Being in a common-law or spousal relationship can impact the amount of federal tax you and your partner pay, and can ultimately impact one's income and monetary investments. There exists a spousal tax credit for circumstances where one's common-law partner or spouse has a lower income (Canada Revenue Agency, n.d.-a). If one financially supports their partner and their partner's net income (reported on line 23600 on their return) is less than one's basic personal amount, then one can claim the amount on line 30300 (which was formerly line 303 before the 2019 tax year). Ultimately, the higher-income common-law partner or spouse is considered to be "supporting" the lower-income earning partner and so the higher earner typically claims the tax credit. An additional $2,295 can be claimed if the supported partner has been dependent on their common-law partner or spouse due to a physical or mental impairment or disability. However, only one individual in a relationship can claim the amount on line 30300 during the same tax year. The spousal tax credit is still applicable if one's common-law partner or spouse is a non-resident (TaxTips.ca - Line 30300 Spouse or Common-Law Partner Amount Tax Credit, n.d.). To determine if the non-resident partner is truly being supported by the Canadian partner, the Canada Revenue Agency will review their income, any support provided to the individual from government agencies in their home country (including pensions, housing, etc), the ability of the individual to be self-supporting or cost of living in the country of their residence, and any support provided by individuals aside from the Canadian partner.

Common-law and married couples also have the option of pooling several types of expenses when filing their tax returns to potentially receive a larger tax credit. For donations and gifts given to certain institutions, one may be able to federal and provincial or territorial non-refundable tax credits (Canada Revenue Agency, 2017a). Typically, one can claim all or part of the eligible amount, up to 75% of one's net income. Qualified institutions and organizations that can receive donations and gifts include registered charities, journalism organizations, Canadian amateur athletic associations, national arts service organizations, Canadian housing organizations for aged populations, municipalities in Canada, the United Nations and its agencies, universities housing Canadian students regularly, a province or territory, or a foreign charity to which The Crown in Right of Canada has made a gift (Canada Revenue Agency, 2017b). Qualified recipients may issue official donation receipts to aid in this process, however, the United Nations, its agencies, The Crown, or a province or territory will not do so as they will automatically qualify. One partner can claim all the couple's charitable donations on their tax return or they can be carried forward and claimed in a larger sum during any of the next 5 years.

Additionally, common-law and married couples can pool their medical expenses with the lower-income earner claiming all the medical expenses for the couple. Medical expenses can only be claimed in a tax year if the payment concluded in that year and if they were not previously claimed, and only the portion of the payment that was not reimbursed (Canada Revenue Agency, 2016). All amounts paid out-of-pocket, including portions paid out of Canada, can be claimed. A large variety of medical expenses are eligible to be claimed including some items that may be unexpected such as air conditioners and air filters, cleaners, or purifiers with a medical prescription, diapers or disposable briefs for persons with incontinence, page-turner devices, and service animals for some disabilities and disorders besides just severe blindness or deafness (Canada Revenue Agency, 2016).

Common-law partners or spouses also can split one's eligible pension income to lower the amount of tax one is required to pay. Pension income splitting can be done for pension income from the taxable part of life annuity payments from a superannuation or pension fund or plan or pension income received from a deceased common-law partner or spouse (Canada Revenue Agency, 2007). Old age security payments, the Canada Pension Plan and the Quebec Pension Plan, and income from an individual retirement account in the United States are all ineligible for pension income splitting. Furthermore, the age of one's common-law partner or spouse does not impact the ability to split pension-related income.

The role of children in tax forms

It is no surprise that raising children today is an expensive and demanding task, and so the need to address these costs and support Canadian families is apparent. The Canada Child Benefit, a tax-free monthly payment intended to help with costs associated with raising children below the age of 18, is organized and provided by the Canada Revenue Agency (Canada Revenue Agency, 2020). To receive this benefit, one must live with a child under 18, be primarily responsible for the child's care and upbringing, and be a Canadian resident (Canada Revenue Agency, 2020). When two parents are equally involved in the child's care, it is assumed that the female parent is the primary caregiver and is recommended to apply for the benefit. This is a legislative requirement despite holding many assumptions regarding the role of women in the family unit and society that one might argue do not reflect the values held by many Canadians today. It is specified for same-sex parents that only one parent should apply for each child had by the couple (Canada Revenue Agency, 2020). One can apply for the benefit anytime after the child is born, when a child begins living with an individual, or when custody is awarded. There are also specific practices in place for persons seeking the Canada Child Benefit whilst leaving an abusive or violent situation, to ensure the safety of all family members.

Child care expenses, which are necessary for a parent or guardian to work, run a business, attend school, or carry on specific research projects, can also be claimed in part (Canada Revenue Agency, 2004a). An eligible child for which care expenses can be claimed is under 16 years of age at some point in the tax year and is either one or one's spouse or common-law partner's child or a child dependent whose net income for the year is $13,808 or less (Canada Revenue Agency, 2004a). Claims can include traditional child care services, daycare centres, but also educational institutions that have fees related to child care, various day camps, boarding schools, and camps where lodging is provided (Canada Revenue Agency, 2004b). Care provided by a relative under the age of 18 or a parent cannot be claimed (Canada Revenue Agency, 2004a).

Adoption-related expenses can also be claimed, up to $16,729 per child, but it must be claimed at the end of the period for the year in which the adoption occurred or was recognized by the Canadian government (Canada Revenue Agency, 2004c). Fees related to this process can include fees paid directly to the adoption agency, court costs and legal and administrative expenses related to the adoption order, necessary travel expenses, document translation fees, mandatory fees paid for a child's immigration, and any mandatory fees paid to a foreign institution (Canada Revenue Agency, 2005).

Differences in Cost and Taxation Based on Gender

It is a reality of the world today that there are differences in products marketed toward men and women. From the bright and colourful packaging and descriptive titles to the cost of products, there exist markups on clothing, toiletries and healthcare products, and other items which people purchase regularly. This difference in gender-based pricing is frequently called "the pink tax", and while there is no intentional taxation on feminine products, this trend in increased pricing for traditionally feminine products has continued since the 1990s (Najdenovska, n.d.). While one can recognize the unfairness of differing prices based on appearances and not substantial differences in the product in terms of content, quality, or delivery, there are further concerns about the implications of the pink tax. It, in part, robs women of agency of choice while implying that they can be swayed by the pretty packaging and fun scents so much that they would pay more for one product over one that is inherently the same. In this section of the chapter, the impacts of gendered pricing, and the history of additional taxation of feminine hygiene products in the United States and Canada.

In addition to the pink tax, a separate trend in taxing feminine hygiene products has been referred to as the "tampon tax" where these products are taxed as "luxury goods" despite being necessary for anyone who menstruates (Hunter, 2016). Feminine hygiene products, including pads, tampons, panty liners, menstrual cups, and menstrual discs, were not recognized as "necessary goods" in Canada until 2015 when the Canadian Parliament first started the process to exempt period products from the higher tax. Previous to this, the Goods and Services Tax ("GST") had certain exemptions for items such as basic food and groceries and medical supplies. GST was first introduced by the Conservative federal government in 1991 under the Excise Tax Act (Scala, 2022). Being a consumption sales tax, the responsibility of GST falls on the consumer at the time of purchase rather than the seller of the goods. GST is currently 5%, but in provinces with an additional Provincial Sales Tax ("PST"), it becomes a larger percentage of every purchase with the combined Harmonized Sales Tax ("HST") (Canada Revenue Agency, n.d.-a). Items exempt from GST in Canada currently include select food items, prescription medications, music lessons, wedding cakes, and even cocktail cherries (Scala, 2022).

The announcement of the end to the tampon tax in Canada was made by the Conservative government of the time on May 28th, 2015. This coincides with being the official day for Menstrual Hygiene which is an awareness initiative that is promoted globally (Scala, 2022). Months previously, the New Democratic Party (NDP) had introduced a motion to end the tampon tax after many previous failed attempts to do so. The actual issue of additional tax on period products predates the establishment of GST, with provincial taxes targeting items in the 1980s in Ontario. The finance minister's 1982 list of items to be included in tax exemption excluded any hygiene products specific to women in an act that was criticized to be thereby directly taxing women in the province. Only three years later, Liberal premier David Peterson ensured that feminine hygiene products were moved to the list of exempted items. When GST was introduced in the 90s, concerns about the taxation of period products were almost immediate. A couple of Ontario women presented a petition to the minister responsible for women's issues that received 50,000 signatures while an Albertan woman hired a lawyer to make a case for sexual discrimination under the Canadian Charter of Rights and Freedoms. While the case was unable to progress due to a lack of funding, it speaks to the extent to which women advocates worked to oppose federal taxation of necessary items related to their health and the health of anyone who menstruates. A primary interest group acting in 2015 was Canadian Menstruators ("CM"), who campaigned for an end to the tampon tax and increased accessibility and affordability of period products (Canadian Menstruators, n.d.). A lot of their online campaigns pitted tampons against Viagra, the brand name prescription drug prescribed for erectile dysfunction, of which the latter was excluded from federal tax despite the option to engage in sexual activity compared to the inability to decide anything around menstruation. How the NDP spoke about the tampon tax in parliament focussed on the discriminatory nature of the tax on feminine hygiene products and how it increasingly impacted low-income, unhoused women, and women living in remote northern communities as a forced-upon financial burden (Scala,

2022). Ultimately, the GST exemption for feminine hygiene products was the most favoured solution to address equity for persons who menstruate for both interest groups like CM and the NDP and was further supported by the Conservative Party of Canada for their desire and preferences for tax cuts.

In the United States ("US"), sales tax only varies by state with there being no federal tax that applies to all states. As seen with some exemptions in Canada, some states have bizarre items with tax exemptions such as marshmallows in Florida and snowmobiles in Maine (Wakeman, 2018). Currently, in the US, 36 states still have luxury taxes being applied to period products that when needed every month for 40 years adds up to a significant amount of money being demanded of menstruators (Zraick, 2019). The state of New Jersey officially eliminated the tampon tax in 2005, relatively early compared to other states (Sagner, 2018). Prices faced by consumers after the decision to eliminate the state tax (which was 6.9 per cent at the time and is now 6.625 per cent) decreased by 7.3 per cent (Cotropia & Rozema, 2018; NJ Division of Taxation - Sales and Use Tax, n.d.).

Criticisms of repealing tampon taxes in different political environments around the world tend to focus on either the minimal impact of eliminating taxation on a small item or denying that feminine hygiene products themselves are not necessary to use. While the need for these items has previously been spoken of in this chapter, the reality of period poverty has not been. Menstruators who cannot afford to meet their basic needs are seen to continually prioritize feeding themselves over purchasing period products–a decision that anyone facing hunger would be inclined to make (Rafanelli, 2019). People who are unable to access pads and tampons often resort to less sanitary and hygienic options, such as using rags or old t-shirts, making makeshift pads or even tampons using public restroom toilet paper, or free bleeding (Female Homelessness and Period Poverty, 2021; Rafanelli, 2019). Many of the options that these menstruators resort to also leave them more vulnerable to yeast infections and urinary tract infections (Female Homelessness and Period Poverty, 2021). Beyond just the use of pads and tampons, the ability to clean oneself during menstruation is incredibly valuable for one's sanitation and mental health–but people do not yet have universal access to these products let alone the ability to meet additional health-related needs.

Regarding the impact of tax on feminine hygiene products, it is not the best way to improve affordability and access to menstrual hygiene products because they remain a monthly expense. While there is the ability to select between brand options, people with periods still need to choose between where to spend their money and do not have the choice to avoid it based on how our society functions on a day-to-day basis–despite menstrual hygiene products being part of menstruators basic healthcare needs. Despite only marginal differences being made in repealing sales tax for menstrual hygiene products, these decisions do speak to an intentional move to not tax items that disproportionately affect women. However, it has been noted that policies that cover a significant proportion of the cost of menstrual hygiene products will be able to make bigger impacts on the affordability of items (Rafanelli, 2019). This could be implemented through direct subsidies, or as this study was written in the US, allowing food stamps or Medicaid to be used for the purchase of period products, or allowing tax credits for these purchases made over a year. The Supplemental Nutrition Assistance Program ("SNAP"; "food stamps") is an initiative of the US Federal government that allows persons in need to make specific food purchases (Food Assistance, n.d.). Currently, the food stamps program allows the purchase of fruits and vegetables, meat, poultry and fish, dairy, and bread and cereal products with the specific product list provided by the United States Department of Agriculture. Some opponents have even argued that repealing the tampon tax will impact other efforts to increase affordability and access to menstrual hygiene products by exhausting the political capital needed to enact change (Rafanelli, 2019). While these criticisms are valid and have greater concerns with making it possible to get period products into the hands of those who need them the most, the policy move to subsidize period products will impact lower-income individuals while not aiding middle-class individuals who still face these expenses. A combination of having no additional and discriminatory sales tax and improving state or federal initiatives in the US and provincial initiatives in Canada will best address the inherent sex differences in cost associated with menstruating.

References

Canada Revenue Agency. (n.d.-a). Marital status. Retrieved from https://www.canada.ca/en/revenue-agency/services/tax/individuals/topics/about-your-tax-return/tax-return/completing-a-tax-return/personal-address-information/marital-status.html

Canada Revenue Agency. (n.d.-b). Processing spouses and common-law partners: Assessing the legality of a marriage. Retrieved from https://www.canada.ca/en/immigration-refugees-citizenship/corporate/publications-manuals/operational-bulletins-manuals/permanent-residence/non-economic-classes/family-class-determining-spouse/legality.html

Canada Revenue Agency. (2004a). Line 21400 - What are child care expenses? Retrieved from https://www.canada.ca/en/revenue-agency/services/tax/individuals/topics/about-your-tax-return/tax-return/completing-a-tax-return/deductions-credits-expenses/line-21400-child-care-expenses/line-21400-what-child-care-expenses.html

Canada Revenue Agency. (2004b, January 23). Line 21400 - What payments can you claim? Retrieved from https://www.canada.ca/en/revenue-agency/services/tax/individuals/topics/about-your-tax-return/tax-return/completing-a-tax-return/deductions-credits-expenses/line-21400-child-care-expenses/line-21400-what-payments-you-claim.html

Canada Revenue Agency. (2004c). Line 31300 – Adoption expenses. Retrieved from https://www.canada.ca/en/revenue-agency/services/tax/individuals/topics/about-your-tax-return/tax-return/completing-a-tax-return/deductions-credits-expenses/line-31300-adoption-expenses.html

Canada Revenue Agency. (2005). Line 31300 – Adoption expenses: Are your expenses eligible? Retrieved from https://www.canada.ca/en/revenue-agency/services/tax/individuals/topics/about-your-tax-return/tax-return/completing-a-tax-return/deductions-credits-expenses/line-31300-adoption-expenses/your-expenses-eligible.html

Canada Revenue Agency. (2007). Eligible pension income. Retrieved from https://www.canada.ca/en/revenue-agency/services/tax/individuals/topics/pension-income-splitting/eligible-pension-income.html

Canada Revenue Agency. (2016). Lines 33099 and 33199 – Eligible medical expenses you can claim on your tax return. Retrieved from https://www.canada.ca/en/revenue-agency/services/tax/individuals/topics/about-your-tax-return/tax-return/completing-a-tax-return/deductions-credits-expenses/lines-33099-33199-eligible-medical-expenses-you-claim-on-your-tax-return.html

Canada Revenue Agency. (2017a). Line 34900 - Donations and gifts. Retrieved from https://www.canada.ca/en/revenue-agency/services/tax/individuals/topics/about-your-tax-return/tax-return/completing-a-tax-return/deductions-credits-expenses/line-34900-donations-gifts.html

Canada Revenue Agency. (2017b). Which donations can I claim? Retrieved from https://www.canada.ca/en/revenue-agency/services/tax/individuals/topics/about-your-tax-return/tax-return/completing-a-tax-return/deductions-credits-expenses/line-34900-donations-gifts/which-donations-claim.html

Canada Revenue Agency. (2020). Canada child benefit. Retrieved from https://www.canada.ca/en/revenue-agency/services/child-family-benefits/canada-child-benefit-overview.html

Canadian Menstruators (n.d.). About the campaign: the history of the battle for tax fairness. Retrieved from http://www.canadianmenstruators.ca/

Cotropia, C., & Rozema, K. (2018). Who benefits from repealing tampon taxes? Empirical evidence from New Jersey. Journal of Empirical Legal Studies, 15(3), 620–647. Retrieved from https://scholarship.richmond.edu/law-faculty-publications/1503/

Government of the USA (n.d.). Food Assistance. Retrieved from https://www.usa.gov/food-help

Hunter, L. (2016). The "Tampon Tax": Public Discourse of Policies Concerning Menstrual Taboo. Hinckley Journal of Politics, 17(1). Retrieved from https://epubs.utah.edu/index.php/HJP/article/view/2972

National Organization for Women (2021). Female Homelessness and Period Poverty. National Organization for Women. Retrieved from https://now.org/blog/female-homelessness-and-period-poverty/

Najdenovska, A. (n.d.). Pink Tax in Canada: What Is It and Why Does It Exist? Retrieved from https://reviewlution.ca/resources/pink-tax-canada/

Rafanelli, A. (2019). Rags Instead of Tampons. Here's What Period Poverty Looks Like in the U.S. Direct Relief. Retrieved from https://www.directrelief.org/2019/10/rags-instead-of-tampons-heres-what-period-poverty-looks-like-in-the-u-s/

Sagner, E. (2018). More States Move To End "Tampon Tax" That's Seen As Discriminating Against Women. NPR News. Retrieved from https://www.npr.org/2018/03/25/564580736/more-states-move-to-end-tampon-tax-that-s-seen-as-discriminating-against-women

Scala, F. (2022). Menstrual Activism, Insider-Outsider Alliances and Agenda-Setting: An Analysis of the Campaign to End the "Tampon Tax" in Canada. Journal of Women, Politics & Policy, 2021(1), 1–17. doi: 10.1080/1554477X.2022.2081913

State of New Jersey (n.d.). NJ Division of Taxation - Sales and Use Tax. Retrieved from https://www.state.nj.us/treasury/taxation/businesses/salestax/index.shtml

TaxTips (n.d.). Line 30300 Spouse or Common-Law Partner Amount Tax Credit. TaxTips. Retrieved from https://www.taxtips.ca/filing/spousal-amount-tax-credit.htm

Wakeman, J. (2018). The Real Cost of Pink Tax. Healthline. Retrieved from https://www.healthline.com/health/the-real-cost-of-pink-tax

Zraick, K. (2019). "Tampon Tax" Survives Despite Push for Equity. The New York Times. Retrieved from https://www.nytimes.com/2019/07/12/us/tampon-tax.html

Racial and Cultural Implications of Tax

Uncovering the Racial and Ethnic Disadvantage

In many parts of the world, the 21st century continues to uphold racial and ethnic injustices in tax policies at the state or municipal level. This struggle to promote equity amongst different racial and ethnic groups in terms of income and wealth distribution may reflect the unwashable stains of discrimination that have been ravaged through centuries (Institution on Taxation and Economic Policy, 2021). The policies, which have although revised for improvement over the last decades, continue to impose disproportionate forms of precarity on marginalised or minority groups. By leaving some of these racial and ethnic inequalities addressed in their state tax codes, they may, subconsciously or with motivation, solidify inherent biases against certain groups over others (Institution on Taxation and Economic Policy, 2021).

For example, many Black and Hispanic families struggle to grasp or make the most of opportunities to become wealthy landowners or business owners because of supposedly-racist policies such as redlining or lending practice restrictions (Institution on Taxation and Economic Policy, 2021). Redlining, common in the United States, is a discriminatory practice that restricts the allocation of housing loans (and often extended to other types) to certain eligible applicants because of their neighbourhood district; these areas usually contain a large proportion of ethnic or racialized groups (Harris & Forester, 2003). Unfortunately, it is not an easy task for policymakers to choose their policy semantics and syntax in such a manner after fully understanding the impact of their policy.

Cultural taxation, hence, refers to the additional roles and responsibilities that marginalized groups are burdened with to meet their professional needs and goals because of their minority status - determined by ethnicity, religion, sexual orientation, race, etc (Cleveland et al., 2018). This chapter aims to outline the racial and cultural implications of the tax code in terms of the racial wealth gap and the general diversity in workplaces in Canada and the USA. Both are highly developed and multicultural nations of North America that share many similarities at the policy level regarding the tax code. A larger focus is given to the challenges stemming from the United States due to the availability of literature and transference to Canadian challenges. Finally, the chapter will conclude with proposed solutions to close the gaps motivated by the racial and ethnic implications through both policy research and institutional changes in private and public workplaces.

The Racial Wealth Gap

The wealth disparity between white families in North America and any other race of family is tremendous (Williamson, 2020). According to the Survey of Consumer Finances in 2016 reporting finances of families in the USA, the median net worth of white family households is almost ten times greater than that of black family households. Black households are simply underrepresented in the middle-upper class sectors of family income and wealth distribution, indubitably due to job and business opportunities which is to be later explored in this chapter (SCF, 2016). Factors other than education and job income may be responsible for driving these inequalities.

First, consumption taxes - including general sales tax - tends to be one of the key pushing factors for wealth disparity. For most low-to-middle-income families, consumption taxes swallow up an enormous percentage of their annual income. Although white populations are greater in North American than black or other ethnic minority populations, a larger proportion of households of color remain in this lower to middle-income sector (Williamson, 2020). These consumption tax policies limit the amount of savings that Black, Hispanic, Indigenous, or other families of color often have due to their low income, whereas a majority of white families can build their savings over time. The saying "the rich get richer" is brought to light here as these savings can be invested for higher returns (Williamson, 2020).

Restrictions due to consumption and other forms of taxing may lead to other racial and cultural implications that further inequalities, such as through the real estate market. Investment property and housing convey some of the greatest barriers to systemic racism in action in our societies (Imbroscio, 2020). Going off of the mention of redlining, other similar biases penalize colored families at almost every step of the way to buying or renting a house or looking into real estate for investment (Asare, 2022). Conventional attitudes toward racism can be observed when studying the certain geographic and spatial distributions of ethnicities within American and Canadian cities. These enduring modalities have continued over many decades to influence urban housing and spatial patterns that often separate high-end white families from ethnic enclaves of low socioeconomic status (Imbroscio, 2020).

Yet, this problem has persisted and should continue to persist because it is nearly impossible to discern between economic and racial motives in the real-estate market (Imbroscio

2020). There is often a naive viewpoint that supply and demand are the only forces influencing sales and investments. However, the implicit racial biases that influence property values and decisions to sell or not remain unacknowledged. Those that would complain would often be accused of playing the 'race card' as there usually is no concrete evidence to support claims (Imbroscio, 2020). Others may argue that the residents themselves follow the urge to settle into a neighbourhood that contains a large proportion of people of their ethnicity (Wong et al., 2020). For example, a family of immigrants from India may likely choose to situate themselves in an area containing mostly Indian families because they may feel more welcome and familiar with their races. Essentially, this is to argue against or deny the existence of, a racial wage gap based on geographic distribution alone. Note that while this may not always be the case, there is a reliable phenomenon being studied - the own-race bias - that offers some support to this theory. The own-race bias phenomenon rationalises that because people remember faces of their race or ethnicity better than unfamiliar faces of other races or cultures, they may adapt better socially due to an implicit bias. Nevertheless, this rationale does not explain why ethnic or racial enclaves usually tend to have lower median family incomes and associations with low socioeconomic status than affluent Caucasian neighbourhoods (Williamson, 2020).

The racial wealth gap continues to be an outcome of the current tax policies in place in North American societies today. However, many assumptions are being made which may either disguise or exacerbate the real socioeconomic situations (Williamson, 2020). One is the use of the median income and net worth to compare white families to other colored families. Rather, some of the most extreme wealth is concentrated by certain white families (i.e. a higher number of Caucasian billionaires holding a large proportion of the nation's total wealth) and this may overstate the wealth differences between races (Williamson). What is almost certainly true, however, is that current policies lead to not only the exclusion of minority races and ethnicities from opportunities for investment and professional growth but also their systemic exploitation (Williamson, 2020). At the more local level, market values in real estate and other business assets can often be an expression of racist motivations and imaginaries (Imbroscio, 2020). Williamson and Imbroscio both argue that the numerically small number of people in North America that hold the greatest concentration of wealth are White men and that progressive taxation policies can help close this racial wealth gap (2020, 2020).

Diversity in the Workplace

Quite strongly affiliated with the racial wealth gap is the concept of promoting diversity, equity, and inclusion (DEI) in the workplace. DEI initiatives have risen up and gained power and progress over the last decade, especially since the killing of George Floyd in May 2020, which sparked a wave of corporate activism. Although the term 'diversity' may often be thrown around loosely, recognizing diversity can be through various forms such as hiring and training practices, assignment of roles and responsibilities, the reward system, and celebrating culture through different ways to include staff and clients/customers/patients (Cleveland et al., 2018).

Ironically, the term 'cultural taxation' has been coined to describe the form of tax imposed on people belonging to a minority or marginalised group. Needless to expand, this is a discriminatory and racist form of practice that continues to exist subtly and subconsciously in many workplaces as these workers are burdened with additional duties and requirements asked of them (Cleveland et al., 2018). For instance, in higher education such as colleges and universities, faculty members of color are often expected to assist international or immigrant students through mentoring and advising - additional services that are not necessarily listed in job descriptions or eligible for remuneration (Guillaume & Apodaca, 2020). Engagement in these services helps faculty members of color find job satisfaction and more importantly, job security and longevity. Although these additional services help students feel safe and included by having such a diverse staff to support and mentor them, the services primarily serve motivations of promoting the institutions' reputation. Colleges and universities can show that they are attempting to include diversity and inclusion, whereas the real motive of recruiting colored people may be more self-centred (Cleveland et al., 2018); marginalisation and social stigma may remain embedded in the culture of the educational institution and hence, this would not be an effective promotion of diversity.

On a similar note, a study by Guillaume and Apodaca in 2020 summarized this racial discrepancy in education settings. They found that faculty of color often find it much more difficult to achieve workloads and processes that can lead to promotion, tenure, or other forms of job advancement. A rationale for this discrimination is that the additional imposed responsibilities by institutions influence how these teachers engage in principal activities such as "scholarship, teaching, and service endeavours" (Guillaume & Apodaca, 2020). Essentially, faculty members identifying with ethnic or minority faculty members are often overburdened with the additional responsibilities of mentoring and forming support networks or even teaching courses that focus on race and diversity; these have negative repercussions that inhibit productivity.

However, it may be argued that these activities are needed at educational institutions because they are important for meeting the student's social and emotional needs through having faculty members as connections. But, the problem of race is rooted even deeper than that. Guillaume and Apodaca (2020) argue that institutions often presume that faculty of color should be equipped with the knowledge of their cultural differences and can confidently pass on this knowledge through courses, discussions, casual social events, etc. Minority educators should feel obliged to show 'good citizenship' by addressing the institution's needs to showcase itself as ethnically representative. But, this may simply be a reflection of their institution's implicit bias toward these individuals (Guillaume & Apodaca, 2020). Implicit bias in this manner can lead these faculty members to experience discrimination in their workplace, leading to social niches, and ultimately going back to this main issue - the broadening of the racial wealth gap.

Diversity and inclusion in the workplace was a vital section to discuss in this chapter because it connects to the racial and cultural implications of tax policies subtly, yet directly. As many studies investigate the impact of "cultural taxation" that ethnic minorities pay daily at the individual level, the general society can begin raising questions on how institutions truly perceive and treat these members for better retention (Guillaume & Apodaca, 2020). Although implicit bias may continue to remain in some workplaces, raising these questions would guide institutions and policymakers to implement the progressive steps for maintaining racial equity (in terms of tenure and promotions).

Looking at History: The Cumulative Effects on State Economies

Furthermore, the racial and cultural implications of taxation could have devastating effects on state economies as a whole (Leachman et al., 2018). Continuing off of cultural taxation, the inhibition in productivity levels of minority workers that are limited from reaching their true potential indubitably leads to adverse economic effects. When these state residents are held back from making the most of their skills and accessing opportunities, they are hindered in terms of their contributions to their state economy (Leachman et al., 2018).

Affiliated with similar parameters, such as socioeconomic status and median household income between races, the state economy is, in essence, an overall projection of the racial wealth gap (Leachman et al., 2018). In the late 19th to early 20th century, state tax policies were established on the basis that the white race was inherently superior to all others (Leachman et al., 2018). In many parts of America from the late 1800s to 1900s, the Jim Crow Laws deprived African Americans of the right to vote, the "privilege" of running a business, and of their participation in State legislatures. At that period in time, African Americans and other people of color generally held low socioeconomic status with low-paying jobs in the manufacturing or resources sectors or lower-level service positions if they were fortunate (Leachman et al., 2018).

When significant proportions of the population are held back by racial and cultural biases, it should be no surprise that the state economy was lower relative to other states where laws were not as discriminatory. For example, Alabama's government explicitly aimed to assert white dominance by establishing restrictive property tax limits for white landowners (Leachman et al., 2018). These policies were introduced out of fear that even a few people of color would eventually rise to power and cause an increase in tax rates to fund their children's education and well-being. Obviously, most of these laws have been scrapped over time, but the harmful cumulative effects in Alabama are still evident today: Alabama is the state with the lowest property tax revenue as a share percentage of its state economy (Leachman et al., 2018). This may explain the inadequate funding for education and other public services that lead to infrastructural differences in some northern and southern states today.

Therefore, we cannot live with the delusion that because the policies have changed and are not as discriminatory anymore, there is racial equity in taxes and the economy. Today, despite Hispanics, Native Americans, and Asians accounting for close to 25% of the American population, only 7% of State lawmakers identify as being from these minority ethnicities (Leachman et al., 2018). Similarly, African Americans are very much underrepresented in legislative or judiciary state or national affairs relative to their share of the population (Leachman et al., 2018). Hence, even in states that hold people of color as population majorities, white lawmakers may overlook some of the minute details in current policies, some that remain unchanged since the 19th century, leading to the continued assertion of white dominance.

Just as important as tax policy is the factor of how these policies are administered by authorities. For example, African American landowners were often taxed at higher rates as their properties were typically over-assessed compared to their white counterparts (Leachman et al., 2018). Again, it is difficult to discern whether this was performed out of explicit racial discrimination by authorities or out of implict bias, but the effects of these actions also convey cumulative effects toward today's state economies.

Proposed Work

Altogether, the historically cumulative effects of tax policy seem to hold major effects on today's society and implicit attitudes toward people of color in North America. The shaping of demographics, as larger proportions of minority populations belonging to low socioeconomic status reside in ghetto areas with poor provision of public services, seem almost irreversible. Yet, on a positive note, state and national policymakers are scrutinising the policies more intensely than ever to revert this change for enhancing racial equity (Leachman et al., 2018). State fiscal policies and their equitable administration would be perhaps the most powerful force to close down the racial wealth gap, promote diversity and inclusion in public and private institutions, and reduce the poverty of ethnic minorities by promoting more opportunities for economic contributions (Leachman et al., 2018).

One popular solution that has been floating around in Canada and the USA over the past decade is to shift policies based on the ability of the people to pay taxes. Currently, some states or provinces, such as Pennsylvania, have flat-rate income tax rates that agonise the poor and barely prick the rich (Leachman et al., 2018). Some states such as California and North Carolina have begun to take steps to increase the rate of taxation for very high-income households (Leachman et al., 2018). However, neither does this strategy guarantee the mitigation of racial and cultural inequities nor does it identify the roots of the problem - discrimination in policymaking and administration.

Rather, another step that states or provinces could begin to take that is more direct in their method is to introduce Earned Income Tax Credits ("EITCs") (Leachman et al., 2018). EITCs tend to address the currently regressive taxes, such as sales tax, that have disproportionate impacts on people of color. By providing tax credits to low-income household families, usually ethnic minorities, more money is left over after taxes have been deducted. EITCs are particularly renowned in the USA for reducing poverty amongst low-income households of color and offering greater accessibility to services such as child care and transportation (Leachman et al., 2018). Not to mention, this could also reduce other repercussions of poverty such as crime, school and college dropouts, and substance abuse. As policymakers work on editing the current policies, interventions like EITCs would slowly help people of color in poverty achieve stability.

In workplaces, further research should investigate the discriminatory issues associated with cultural taxation and investigate how racially-equitable opportunities can be provided to colored workers to promote more unity in corporate culture (Guillaume & Apodaca, 2020). Policies related to taxation could also be revised to attempt to overcome these underlying systemic inequities that marginalise minorities and hinder them from achieving their true potential. Finally, it is important for governments to better understand how taxation plays perhaps one of the most significant roles in linking race to the economy. By advancing racial equity and closing the racial wealth gaps that may exist at the policy level of taxation, the US and Canada can get one step closer to truly becoming the land of dreams.

References

Asare, J. G. (2022, November 8). How systemic racism is baked into the fabric of American housing. Forbes. Retrieved from https://www.forbes.com/sites/janicegassam/2022/02/01/how-systemic-racism-is-baked-into-the-fabric-of-american-housing/?sh=4600e2a7430f

Cleveland, D. R., Sailes, D. J. D., Gilliam, D. E., & Watts, J. (2018). A theoretical focus on cultural taxation: Who pays for it in higher education. Advances in Social Sciences Research Journal, 5(10). doi: 10.14738/assrj.510.5293

Davis, C., Hill, M., & Wiehe, M. (2021, March 31). Taxes and racial equity: An overview of State and local policy impacts. ITEP. Retrieved from https://itep.org/taxes-and-racial-equity/

Federal Reserve System. (2019). Survey of Consumer Finances. Board of governors of the Federal Reserve System. Retrieved from https://www.federalreserve.gov/econres/scfindex.htm

Guillaume, R. O., & Apodaca, E. C. (2020). Early career faculty of color and promotion and tenure: The intersection of advancement in the Academy and Cultural Taxation. Race Ethnicity and Education, 25(4), 546–563. doi: 10.1080/13613324.2020.1718084

Harris, R., & Forrester, D. (2003). The Suburban Origins of Redlining: A Canadian Case Study, 1935-54. Urban Studies, 40(13), 2661–2686. Retrieved from http://www.jstor.org/stable/43100660

Imbroscio, D. (2020). Race matters (even more than you already think): Racism, housing, and the limits of the color of law. Journal of Race, Ethnicity and the City, 2(1), 29–53. doi: 10.1080/26884674.2020.1825023

Leachman, M., Mitchell, M., Johnson, N., & Williams, E. (2018). Advancing Racial Equity With State Tax Policy. Center on Budget and Policy Priorities. Retrieved from https://www.cbpp.org/research/state-budget-and-tax/advancing-racial-equity-with-state-tax-policy

Williamson, V. (2022, March 9). Closing the racial wealth gap requires heavy, progressive taxation of wealth. Brookings. Retrieved from https://www.brookings.edu/research/closing-the-racial-wealth-gap-requires-heavy-progressive-taxation-of-wealth/

Tax Evasion and Tax Avoidance Methods, Implications, Morality, Economics

This chapter will define and contrast tax evasion and tax avoidance. It will also explore the different potential methods involved in tax evasion as well as the methods that people often practice concerning tax avoidance. Furthermore, this chapter will discuss the direct and indirect implications of tax avoidance and tax evasion. This will include but is not limited to the economic, societal, and political implications of both tax evasion and tax avoidance. Finally, this chapter will explore the morality of taxes, tax avoidance, and tax evasion, from a variety of scopes.

Defining Tax Evasion and Tax Avoidance

Tax evasion, also called tax fraud, can be refined by its most relevant characteristic in contrast with tax avoidance— that it is illegal. Tax evasion characteristically involves hiding or manipulating income and transactional information regarding a person or company's finance, with the end goal of paying fewer taxes to the government (Orem, 2022). It can essentially be summarized as the act of lying about one's finances— whether that be lying about one's income, the volume of one's transactions, or the true nature of one's transactions. On the other hand, tax avoidance, in a general context, is a legal way of optimally displaying a person or company's financial data— without adding false information or subtracting from true information— in a way that minimizes the amount of taxes that must be paid (Orem, 2022). One could potentially argue that in contrast with tax evasion, tax avoidance is not only legal but ethical and perhaps encouraged to a degree (Bass, 2022). This goes especially so for small businesses that require immense financial advisory input to survive the initial rocky stages of a young business. It also applies to the new generation of Canadians entering into the workforce and making a living for themselves; understanding ways to become financially literate, minimize taxes, and build a sustainable financial life plan is important not only to individual economic success but the infrastructural success of a society to a certain degree. However, there are opposing viewpoints that will be discussed later, which question the morality of tax avoidance, with the appreciation of certain nuances.

Methods of Tax Evasion

Given that several different kinds of taxes must be paid by businesses and individuals in different scenarios, tax fraudsters come up with different ways to avoid these particular taxes.

When goods cross certain borders, they are often subjected to border taxes. For example, to protect Canadian dairy producers, any imports of dairy products have to pay sometimes upwards of 200% in taxes. This makes it more costly and less practical for foreign dairy producers to try and penetrate the Canadian dairy market (Khowaja & Kreklewetz, 2021). To get around this, some companies will smuggle their products across the border so that the product is undeclared and never registered as a taxed import, then sell it for profit. Since this contraband is unregistered, it cannot enter the market through normal means. Suppliers must approach sellers that are willing to sell contraband, typically with the temptation of visibly lower supply costs. If caught, both the supplier and local seller can face consequences. Smuggling can also happen on the micro level— due to Canada's controlled cheese market, many foreign cheese types that are not accessible through local channels are taxed at high rates, driving up their prices for consumers. To avoid this, people who travel to those exporting countries often re-enter Canada without declaring the foreign cheese in their possession (Tabak, 2018). This is commonplace and can harm the Canadian dairy industry (or any other industry in question). Customs also demand that a person declares goods to avoid the risk of introducing health hazards, invasive species, and diseases that could put the Canadian population at risk (Government of Canada, 2021).

One of the most common kinds of tax evasion involves filing incorrect income tax returns. This can involve understating one's income to avoid being taxed for that additional income and to avoid being put in a higher tax bracket (Kotak Life, 2022). It can also involve overstating deductions and expenses to claim a greater tax return, or claiming a personal expense to be a business expense since businesses can claim tax returns on their expenses. There are many other kinds of incorrect filings of information that can lead to tax fraud, such as using a false social insurance number, and other such falsifications of information. As a rule of thumb, avoid committing tax fraud by entering information on income tax returns exactly as they are. Businesses must keep a careful record of all their financial information in case they are audited by their federal revenue agency. If an audit concludes that some information was misreported, further action can ensue. Filing incorrect tax information can also include not reporting income whatsoever by not keeping a record of transactions and dealing solely through cash. If a business does not provide invoices for its services, or if a landlord only collects rent through cash payments, this may be an indicator of hiding income from the national revenue agency (Kotak Life, 2022). When businesses provide invoices, it is proof that they at least keep a record of their transactions, since each invoice will have a reference or transaction number that can be used to look it up in the business system.

Another way that people and businesses use to try and evade the line of sight of their country's revenue agency is to create offshore accounts in countries where income is not taxed, or not taxed as severely (Parker, 2022). This is an alternative way of not reporting any taxable income to one's home country since any income made and deposited in a local bank account would be immediately transferred to an offshore account, typically under the pretense of buying pseudo goods (Parker, 2022). This is called a sham transaction, where a business labels a transaction as something it is not, to avoid alerting the law. At the end of the fiscal year, it would appear that the company has a net zero income since any money made was immediately "spent" buying an obscure product from a business located overseas. In reality, that overseas business would be owned by the same person, who can now evade paying high levels of income tax while also retaining all of their locally generated income. The goods in question did not exist, but were simply a manipulation of the nature of the transaction, disguising a suspiciously large and constant transfer of money from one account to another as an innocent but large purchase of goods (Parker, 2022). Note that offshore accounts tread the line between legal tax avoidance and illegal tax fraud. with the key difference being that one must comply with the law and report their offshore accounts to their home country, with all transactions appearing as they are in reality. In the US, people are legally required to report any money exceeding an amount of USD $10,000 to be taxed as normal income. The exception to this is any income that is genuinely earned internationally, which will be subject to the United States' foreign-earned tax exclusion. Even after declaring that income, offshore accounts can have some remaining and completely legal benefits, some of which are not even related to tax avoidance at all (Parker, 2022).

One example of how offshore accounts can legally benefit individuals and businesses is through the stability of that foreign country. For businesses located in politically or economically unstable countries, a sudden collapse or economic depression could cause them to lose all their capital without any warning (Parker, 2022). This could even include anything from civil war to the corruption of their government. Keeping money offshore allows for added protection since their government would have added barriers to seizing or freezing the contents of their overseas bank accounts. Another completely legal advantage of offshore accounts is the facilitation and increased opportunity for international investing (Parker, 2022).

Lastly, the most straightforward method of tax evasion is to simply refuse to pay one's taxes. This is far from a smart idea since even a quick audit will allow one's revenue agency to know that they are committing tax evasion. While an individual may be able to run from the law for a certain time before getting caught, it is far more difficult to dodge the law as a business (Kotak Life, 2022).

Methods of Tax Avoidance

Before continuing with this section, it is important to note that tax avoidance and tax evasion can be difficult to distinguish, especially if a person is not well-versed in the law. As such, it is unwise for someone to attempt tax avoidance without fully comprehending the law in advance. Tax evasion is a crime that affects everyone, so it is crucial to properly follow the laws that one's country has set in place to protect its people.

As another disclaimer to this section, tax avoidance requires planning and detailed forecasting of income. A certain tax planning strategy may reduce taxes for the current year but may increase one's taxes for the following years. Furthermore, a certain strategy that may reduce taxes at a certain level of income can have the opposite effect at a different level of income.

There are many unique ways to avoid taxes that will not be covered explicitly in this chapter. However, three main principles are reflected in most methods of tax avoidance, regardless of the country. These include maximizing tax deductions and tax credits, minimizing taxable income, and lastly, optimizing the timing of income and deductions (Wolters Kluwer, 2020).

As the first item on this list, a tax deduction is defined as an item, usually, an expense, that reduces the portion of income that is taxable. Common tax deductions in Canada include money put towards an RRSP, child or spousal care, and registered pension plans (Cocoves, 2022). It is wise to report all of these deductions to avoid paying taxes on income that is eligible to be exempt from taxation. The difference between deductions and credits is that a tax deduction reduces the portion of income that is considered taxable, whereas a tax credit directly reduces a person's total income tax (Cocoves, 2022). Another crucial difference is that a dollar's worth of tax credit will deduct a dollar's worth of tax, whereas a dollar's worth of tax deductions will deduct one's tax by a rate dependent on which tax bracket a person's income is situated in (Wolters Kluwer, 2020). To illustrate this difference, imagine a man with a pie that has twelve slices, each worth one dollar. The pie represents a person's total income— perhaps out of those twelve slices, the man's neighbour will take a bite out of ten of the slices. The ten slices would be a person's taxable portion of their income. If the man was to claim two slices worth of tax deductions, it would mean that their taxable income is instead eight slices. This would mean that the man's neighbour is only allowed to take a bite out of eight of the twelve slices. This would effectively save the pie man a certain amount of pie since the neighbour is eating two bites less. Alternatively, if he were to claim two slices worth of tax credits, it would instead mean that the ten slices are still available for the neighbour to take a bite out of, but overall, the neighbour must eat two slices less. This analogy illustrates that tax credits are often more effective than deductions for tax avoidance. In the first example, the man saved two bites worth of pie, whereas, in the second example, he saved two whole slices worth.

Given the incredibly direct benefit of tax credits, they are typically only offered to businesses to encourage them to spend on things such as health insurance for employees, or accessibility initiatives. On the other hand, although tax deductions may not always be as impactful, claiming enough deductions can lower a person's taxable income to the point where it fits into the previous bracket. To elaborate, a person or business' income is taxed in progressive brackets, where the first few thousand may be taxed at a low rate, and the next few thousand are taxed at a higher rate. Being able to clear the upper dollars from a higher tax rate can be quite impactful (Wolters Kluwer, 2020).

Asides from maximizing tax deductions, there are other ways of reducing taxable income. A person can time when they perform transactions such as collections, dividends, and capital gains that give rise to tax liability, or the total amount of payable tax to avoid paying more taxes during a certain period. Delaying income receipts to the next year can allow a person to register that income as part of the next year, which can be useful if that makes the difference between tax brackets. However, this is typically only possible with cash transactions, since delaying the reporting of any other method of payment will usually constitute tax evasion. Contrarily, prioritizing deductible expenses so that they are reported before the new year is another good way of claiming more deductibles and reducing tax liability (Wolters Kluwer, 2020).

It should be noted that this strategy is only effective if a person or business is forecasting that they will be in a lower tax bracket in the following year— hence why tax avoidance requires deep planning. One could analogise it to having several buckets, representing fiscal years, and redistributing the water in between them so that it is not overflowing in any of the buckets. This means that reverse logic is also applicable. If a business projects that it will be in a higher bracket next year, it is in its best interests to report income as early as possible, so that that income is taxed within a lower bracket.

To conclude this section, it is important to once again emphasize that improper implementation of tax avoidance can result in audits and other issues with federal revenue agencies.

Morality and Implications of Tax Avoidance

While the illegality of tax evasion considerably removes arguments for it being morally justifiable, certain loopholes that politicians and businesses deliberately exploit are up for debate. While these actions may be considered legal, one must also consider the "big picture". In these instances, the avoidance of tax can have significant consequences from the lens of national revenue, and the benefits that citizens can reap as a result. Anything from healthcare services offered by the government, to student loan plans, and education projects can be affected when people begin to exploit federal tax laws.

Starting with the broadest concepts of ethics, it is important to consider the idea that the classification of something being legal or illegal may not directly translate to that same thing being moral or immoral. However, given the goal of enacting laws, at least in Canada, which is to protect the rights and peace of its Citizens, it would be an ideal situation if laws corresponded as closely as possible to morals. Then again, it is important to recognise that the idea of morality and its subjectivity is a far greater and more ancient debate than that of tax laws. This section will briefly outline the morality of tax avoidance from a few perspectives that are applicable within the context. As a disclaimer, the fact that any of these ethical systems have been given a platform in this chapter does not mean that they are fully endorsed and justified. Ethical systems are uniquely looked upon by different people, and thus not everyone will agree to a certain statement about morality. This, however, does not stop us from holding dialogue and comparing diverse perspectives to gain a better understanding of what is right and what is not. With that being said, it is a fairly universal goal of ethics systems to be able to define and protect everyone's rights in the best way possible.

An ethics system that is popular in today's society is utilitarianism or consequentialism, which constitutes that the moral action is that which causes the greatest good to come about for the greatest number of people that can be involved (Bass, 2022). This kind of ethics system can justify unfortunate tradeoffs as long as the overall benefit outweighs the harm. As applied to tax avoidance, this creates a very tabulated perspective. On the individual level, a higher profile individual who would cost the government a significant amount of money each year by fully exploiting loopholes in tax laws would be benefiting themselves, but taking away funding from institutions that benefit the masses (Filho, 2014).

On the other hand, a low-profile individual who has little to no effect on the grand scheme of things could justify their tax avoidance from a utilitarian perspective, since they are benefiting themselves and harming no one. An interesting point is added when shifting from an individual perspective to a group perspective. Articles and resources that encourage and instruct about tax avoidance can reach large numbers of people, causing increased trends of tax avoidance and taking away money from the aforementioned institutions (Filho, 2014). From a utilitarianist lens, the key question to ask is: are these people benefiting more from avoiding taxes than they would from enjoying that taxpayer money going toward the public sector? It should be noted that utilitarianism can also justify tax evasion, given that the good that is achieved is greater than the good sacrificed.

Another ethical system that can be analyzed under the context of tax avoidance is the deontological system of ethics, which emphasizes the importance of following rules that are set in place by society, under the expectation that everyone will follow them to create a morally and otherwise functional society (Bass, 2022). As such, a deontologist's understanding of moral and immoral corresponds directly with the local understanding of legal and illegal respectively. In brief terms, this would mean that tax avoidance is wholly justified without exceptions, and tax evasion is wholly unjustified. This type of ethics system overlaps with certain religious ethics systems, due to its nature of approach in this context. For example, Islam details its own detailed and complete set of tax laws as a proponent of Islamic law. Given that these laws are assumed to be sent down by a perfect God, anything that is outlawed in this set of tax laws would automatically be considered immoral (McGee, 1970).

Finally, Aristotle's virtue ethics focuses on the internal intent to avoid human vices and strive towards the best person they can be, as defined by Aristotle's virtues or any other justified virtues that a person may hold (Bass, 2022). This is by far the broadest and most subjective ethics system to be applied in this context since an individual's specific actions would need to be evaluated at that moment for how virtuous they could be considered towards themselves. For example, is delaying the reporting of income an instance of being dishonest? Is employing family for the sake of paying them salaries that would duck under higher tax brackets considered unfair nepotism?

Conclusion

Aside from the morality of tax evasion and tax avoidance, it is important to understand the differences and methods, of living in a society that is undoubtedly governed by certain laws. Financial literacy is crucial for bringing more of the population out of the poverty line and improving the overall quality of life within a country.

References

Bass, E. (2022, October 25). Is tax avoidance ethical? asking for a friend. The Conversation. Retrieved from https://the-conversation.com/is-tax-avoidance-ethical-asking-for-a-friend-147967

Cocoves, A. (2022, August 16). What are tax deductions? NerdWallet Canada. Retrieved from https://www.nerdwal-let.com/ca/personal-finance/what-are-tax-deductions

Filho, R. (2014, December). The ethics of tax avoidance - George Washington University. The Ethics of Tax Avoid-ance. Retrieved from https://www2.gwu.edu/~ibi/minerva/Fall2014/Ronaldo_Parreira.pdf

Government of Canada, C. B. S. A. (2021, August 27). Govern-ment of Canada. Government of Canada, Canada Border Services Agency. Retrieved from https://www.cbsa-asfc.gc.ca/services/fpa-apa/regs-eng.html

Khowaja, S. & Kreklewetz, R. (2021). Importing cheese & dairy into Canada – TRQ required! Tax and Trade Law. Re-trieved from https://www.taxandtradelaw.com/Tax-Trade-Blog/importing-cheese-dairy-into-canada-trq-required.html

Kotak Life. (2022, June 16). What is tax evasion and what are the penalties for tax evasion in India? Kotak Life. Retrieved from https://www.kotaklife.com/insurance-guide/saving-stax/what-is-tax-evasion-and-what-are-the-penalties-for-tax-evasion-in-india

McGee, R. W. (1970, January 1). Tax evasion in Islam. Sprin-gerLink. Retrieved from https://link.springer.com/chapter/10.1007/978-1-4419-9140-9_7#citeas

Orem, T. (2022, September 15). Tax evasion and tax avoidance: Definitions & differences. NerdWallet. Retrieved from https://www.nerdwallet.com/article/taxes/tax-evasion-vs-tax-avoidance

Parker, T. (2022, July 8). Offshore banking isn't illegal but hiding it is. Investopedia. Retrieved from https://www.investopedia.com/articles/managing-wealth/042916/offshore-banking-isnt-illegal-hiding-it.asp

Tabak, N. (2018, March 2). What turns some law-abiding Canadians into smugglers? The high price of imported cheese. The World from PRX. Retrieved from https://theworld.org/stories/2018-03-02/what-turns-some-law-abiding-canadians-smugglers-high-price-imported-cheese

Wolters, K. (2020, November 6). Tax avoidance is legal; tax evasion is criminal. Wolters Kluwer. Retrieved from https://www.wolterskluwer.com/en/expert-insights/tax-avoidance-is-legal-tax-evasion-is-criminal

Can We Have a Universal Basic Income?

Introduction

When a large number of Canadians lost their jobs as a result of the COVID-19 pandemic, many of those same people were able to take advantage of the federal government's Canada Emergency Response Benefit (CERB). This benefit provided eligible Canadians who applied a monthly sum of money to pay their living expenses for a short time period while they were out of work (Service Canada, 2022). The program reignited conversations in the media about a universal or guaranteed basic income system for Canadians and whether it would work. Before we can attempt to answer whether or not we can have a universal basic income (UBI), it is important to understand what it is, its history, how it works, who it impacts, as well as many other considerations these conversations center on. This chapter examines these considerations with examples from other countries and opinions from experts in related fields.

What is Universal Basic Income?

In Canada, there are government-sponsored programs in place to provide for those who need income assistance, but what differentiates a universal basic income program from these are its eligibility requirements. Globally, the parameters for each country's programs are not all the same from country to country, but some features are generally shared worldwide. The Basic Income Earth Network (BIEN, n.d.) outlines five specific defining characteristics of a universal basic income. First, there are regular payments that are issued consistently, as opposed to it being lump-sum or one-time payments. The second characteristic is that it is cash equivalent. In other words, receivers are not paid with vouchers, coupons, or any other methods that would limit what they can get in exchange. Third, each individual is paid rather than grouping households as a single entity. Fourth, it is universal, meaning it is for anyone and everyone regardless of their employment status, health conditions, assets, and earnings, which ties into the last characteristic of it being unconditional. Unlike employment insurance benefits or other social assistance programs, there would be no requirements to work or to be actively looking for work. Obtaining or maintaining any employment with a basic income would be a personal choice (BIEN, n.d.).

Evelyn Forget, a Canadian Health economist based in Manitoba supports the program. In a CBC news article, she outlines the two different types of basic income: universal basic income (UBI) and guaranteed basic income (GBI). Universal basic income would provide everyone with the same benefit amount whereas the guaranteed basic income provides an amount to those with a lower income. The intention for the guaranteed basic income is that no one would earn below a certain amount; their income would be supplemented to bring it up to a minimum amount (Bernstien, 2021).

A Brief History of Universal Basic Income

BIEN (n.d.) provides a history of basic income on its website. They trace the origins of UBI back to the late 18th century. The idea resurfaced in the mid-19th century and has continued to be a topic of debate around the world ever since. Remember, BIEN's definition of UBI means that payments are unconditional, but the idea of a minimum or guaranteed income with conditions attached has been around for much longer. Thomas More's book Utopia, published in 1516 introduces the idea that if the poor were receiving sufficient means to survive, they would be less likely to steal to eat, though they would have to earn those means through labour. This idea moves a step further with Johannes Ludovicus Vives who, in 1526, suggested that these funds be provided through public assistance programs, keeping the caveat that the recipients are willing to work. These ideas continued through the centuries and were the precursor to many of the social assistance programs we have today (BIEN, n.d.).

Who Supports Universal Basic Income?

Cult MTL (2021) reports the results of a study conducted by the Angus Reid Institute to gather opinions of Canadians by province on whether or not they support a system that would implement a universal basic income. According to the results, almost 60% of Canadians are in favour of a program of up to an annual income of $30,000. By province, the highest support comes from the provinces east of Manitoba. The only province not in favour of such a program in Alberta. Results were also categorized by voting affiliation. Participants who voted Liberal or NDP came in for support of the system at 78% and 84%, respectively, and those who voted Conservative came in at only 26% support.

Jaela Bernstien, a journalist for CBC News, accounts for the position of each of Canada's political party leaders on a universal basic income program, as of 2021. She reports that Annamie Paul of the Green Party and Jagmeet Singh of the NDP endorse platforms that support a UBI program. While Justin Trudeau, our current Prime Minister and leader of the Liberal party does not endorse a platform that is outwardly committed to a program, there is support for it from Liberal Members of Parliament. The People's Party of Canada led by Maxime Bernier, the Conservative party, now led by Pierre Poilievre, and the Bloc Québécois's leader Yves-François Blanchet all have platforms that do not commit to UBI (Bernstien, 2021).

When has Canada Tried Universal Basic Income?

Canada has had two short-lived programs involving basic income: in the 1970s in Manitoba and more recently, the Ontario Basic Income Pilot, which was terminated in 2018. Both of these were designed as experiments to address poverty but also sought to understand how basic income impacts willingness to work.

In the mid-1970s, a small rural community in Manitoba experimented with a pilot called Mincome. In an article examining the results of the experiment, Simpson et al. (2017) outline the details of how the program was designed, how participants were selected, and why the program was terminated. They note that the project was in place from 1975-1978 and its intended to find a way to solve the social issue of poverty. The leaders of both the provincial and federal governments agreed to a budget for the experiment, formally called the Basic Annual Income Experiment Project. The questions the project wanted to answer were regarding the effects of this system in terms of both economic and community impacts. What the researchers of this experiment were specifically looking at was labour supply. Collins Dictionary (2022) defines labour supply as, "the total number of hours that workers are willing and able to be paid wages to work for" (np.) In other words, they were looking to determine what impact providing a basic income would have on the individuals' openness to look for work even though they were receiving guaranteed income. They also hoped to address the "logistical challenges involved in implementing such a system across the population" (p. 86).

Simpson et al. (2017) explained the process of how participants were selected. To summarize: the sample started with a total of 1255 low-income families who were selected to receive various allocations of monthly allowances with different tax rates, with one control group that would not be receiving payments. These participants were selected based on a series of eligibility parameters set by the researchers. Data was collected from the participants in the form of self-reporting through surveys and reports conducted three times per year throughout the three-year experiment period. Another group from Dauphin was selected where there were no eligibility requirements; this group is referred to as a "saturation" group. Everyone who applied was accepted.

The program ended in 1978, but the data collected was never fully analysed. The budget was not enough to cover the administration staff needed to interpret the data in a manner that was congruent with the standards of a research experiment. In other words, it could have resulted in incomplete results if shortcuts are taken due to the rising costs of the experiment. The data is currently available to interested researchers in digitized form through the University of Manitoba (Simpson et al. 2017).

The second basic income experiment took place in Ontario, beginning in 2016. It ended as quickly as it began, from the first payment issued in 2017 to the 2018 election of a Conservative government which soon after, canceled the program. Mendelson (2019) notes that the experiment's design is what led to its demise and that to conduct a successful experiment, it is important to look to the Ontario Basic Income Pilot (OBIP) for guidance on what to do and what not to do. He notes that the Mincome saturation group is essential in understanding the effects on the entire community because not only is everyone in that group eligible, but everyone in that group also knows everyone is eligible. In other words, the playing field is equal and there is more transparency between the groups of people. Moreover, this group is a good indicator of what an actual UBI program would produce in results as opposed to a pilot or experiment that excludes community members based on certain eligibility requirements.

Another design flaw that Mendelson (2019) points out is that the income amounts the participants would be receiving are based on their previous year's tax return which does not always necessarily reflect the current financial situation of any individual or household. He also reports that the sample size was small and excluded seniors and that the program only sought to test one tax rate, which again, could produce insufficient data. His report on OBIP outlines the lessons learned from this short-lived experiment in great detail and he provides alternatives in the methodology, should anyone from anywhere in the world decide that a basic or guaranteed income pilot or experiment be conducted (Mendelson, 2019).

Where Else Can We Find Universal Basic Income?

In 2020, Sigal Samuel, a Senior Reporter for Vox, compiled a list of all countries that have participated in a basic income program, whether it is a guaranteed basic income or a universal basic income. The countries include the United States, Canada, Brazil, Finland, Germany, Spain, the Netherlands, Iran, Kenya, Namibia, India, China, and Japan.

Though the general definition of universal basic income

means that the funds are received unconditionally, some of these countries on this list have implemented a program where the funds are conditional. Samuel (2020) states that they are included in this list based on the fact that they have a cash-transfer system in place to address the issue of poverty. For example, one of Brazil's programs mandates that recipients ensure their children attend school and that they have regular visits for health check-ups. Another example is Spain, where the program in place had three different plans within. One of those plans required recipients to either partake in programs that helped train them for employment and/or entrepreneurship a program that required their homes to be refurbished, or some other requirement for them to be involved in community service. The Netherlands had a similar program with conditional community service work for some (Samuel, 2020).

Most of the countries on this list implemented these systems on an experimental basis. Some cases saw a one-time payment, and the rest were monthly. The two countries providing a one-time payment were Hong Kong in 2011 and Japan in 2020. In these two cases, the one-time lump sum payment does not meet BIEN's definition of universal basic income, but they are included on this list for the same reason as the countries where conditions were attached: they were in place as an effort to find solutions to poverty. Some of these experiments were government sponsored while others were social experiments implemented by wealthy individuals. For example, one of Germany's experiments was funded by private donors and Japan's experiment was put forth by billionaire Yusaku Maezawa by way of social media. Others were funded by non-profit organizations such as UNICEF for India's experiment (Samuel, 2020).

While some of these programs were simply experimental, or temporary, some were in place with the intention of it becoming permanent. For example, after Brazil's experiments with a basic income system in the 1990s and again from 2008-2014, a new program was put into place which translates to Citizen's Basic Income. This program is expected to be in place indefinitely. The region of Macao, China has had a program in place since 2008 and Iran's program has been ongoing since 2011. In the United States, both Alaska and North Carolina have had programs in place for many years, Alaska since 1982 and North Carolina since 1997. Kenya's experiment is still ongoing, but it is not intended to be permanent. It was scheduled for 12 years, beginning in 2016 (Samuel, 2020).

Why We Should or Should Not Have Universal Basic Income

In this section, the advantages and disadvantages of implementing a universal basic income are addressed. The following is based on the results of the experiments conducted in the countries where a system of basic income has been piloted, whether short-term or ongoing and from expert opinions in both Canada and the United States.

An interview with two university professors, Fabian Wendt and Doug MacKay outlined some of the pros and cons and what it would mean to both residents receiving the payments and to members of the community as a result of an announcement that their city may be partaking in such a program. Both Wendt and MacKay studied UBI through the University of North Carolina. Ward (2021), prefaces the interview transcript, noting that Steve Schewel, mayor of Durham, North Carolina notified residents that their city might be selected to participate in a social experiment on guaranteed income financed by Twitter CEO, Jack Dorsey. Schewel belongs to a coalition group of mayors who support guaranteed income (Ward, 2021).

In the interview, Wendt, and MacKay comment on the positive effects, this money would have on women. Wendt stated that mothers would benefit by being able to pay for childcare when they need to be working and that an abusive relationship could be easier to leave with money that is otherwise allocated for other needs or is simply unavailable. MacKay comments further that though UBI is not the solution to the concern of income inequality, that extra money could alleviate some stress about it. Both professors cited the two Canadian pilot projects in Manitoba (Mincome) and Ontario when asked if there was evidence a basic income program could work (Ward, 2021).

The Mincome experiment, along with other experiments that took place in the United States in the late 1960s to early 1970s were analysed by Evelyn Forget, a Canadian Health Economist. She outlines some of the advantages in terms of education and provides explanations for why there may be a negative impact on labour supply. Forget (2011), explains that women were able to extend their maternity leave and therefore took longer to return to work, reducing the overall work effort among female participants. She suggests that the male participants' reduction in work effort could be a result of adolescent males favouring continuing their education instead of entering the workforce at a younger age. Other encouraging observations were that elementary school children performed well on tests. Forget's observations of the data on the impacts on physical and mental health using the health administration data from the Mincome experiment. She also cites several studies in which researchers found a strong relationship between poor health and poverty, so strong that it is possibly the greatest reason for poor health, though the exact effects are not fully known. In her analysis of the Mincome data, she found that the rate of hospitalization for accidents, injuries, and mental health admissions reduced over the experiment period (Forget, 2011).

When considering the disadvantages, MacKay points out that there could be an issue of reciprocity. Some public assistance benefits in the United States require recipients to be willing to work in some capacity and some Americans feel this is the way any of these programs should work, including healthcare programs. With UBI, the intention is that it is unconditional. As

144

a result, the programs could be funded through income taxes of those who are working and some feel this is not necessarily equitable. MacKay reminds us that there are valuable contributions these folks make to society that do not have a monetary value that some folks who are part of the labour market may not also be making. For example, not all those who are working are also caring for family members or those less fortunate. Another weakness suggested by Wendt to the program is that there is no benefit to the wealthy with a program meant to target issues of poverty (Ward, 2021). Though the taxation systems between Canada and the United States do not necessarily operate entirely the same, there is an explanation. Evelyn Forget clarifies that in Canada, those who are receiving the benefit but who do not need it would simply return it when they file their income taxes the following year (Bernstien, 2021).

David Green, a professor at the University of British Columbia's Vancouver School of Economics and a labour economist acted as chair for the B.C. Basic Income Panel. This panel was a team of experts who were tasked with assessing the practicality of a basic income program for the province of British Columbia. He spoke to CBC news, commenting that "sending people a cheque and hoping they will do better is not going to answer the problem" (Bernstien, 2021 n.p.). The assessment, conducted by Green et al. unveiled arguments the experts agreed were disadvantages. In the executive summary of their findings, they note that one of these disadvantages is that a basic income program is too costly. They claim that any of the positive outcomes resulting from basic income experiments like starting businesses or continuing education are difficult to prove overall because they would need more than five years of data to sufficiently evaluate the claims.

Furthermore, they state that programs already in place would be superior in achieving those outcomes. Another disadvantage they raised was concerning labour supply. They assert, like others who do not support a basic income program, that receiving a guaranteed regular payment would discourage participants from working. Their suggestion to counter this is to implement regulations regarding wages and working conditions that would incentivise a potential workforce. They also expressed concerns about the impact on society. They feel British Columbians have cultivated a "just society" by being community-minded, valuing reciprocity and dignity and that a basic income program would oppose these ideals because its approach highlights individual autonomy. They conclude that reciprocity is the fundamental goal and that changes to current programs are the best course of action in creating a just society (Green et al., 2020).

Wendt and MacKay discuss some of the concerns that arise when thinking about this type of program. People want to know what amount of money is reasonable for regular payments, how it is financed, and whether other social assistance programs would remain intact if a guaranteed income program were implemented (Ward, 2021).

Conclusion

Knowing that the concept of a universal basic income has been in existence for centuries and that there have been some successes in various experimental and pilot projects designed to test the feasibility of such a program, the question remains: can we have a universal basic income? Though many countries have tested out a basic income system, the answer to that question is not as simple as a hard yes or no. Full transparency is needed when discussing the possibility of options for a UBI program. People need to have their concerns addressed in terms of where the money is coming from, and how the community at large will be impacted by a UBI program. We need to be able to have data from social experiments that demonstrate what a real-life UBI system would look like, conducted over a longer time period than budgets would likely be able to finance.

It should also be clear what type of program is being considered because some programs that do not meet a standard definition of UBI are often cited as though they are the same. The reasons behind some of the pilot projects or social experiments are reported to be primarily in addressing poverty, yet a lot of them exclude populations that have a lower income. The goal of some of the experiments we looked at in this chapter was to see how receiving regular monthly payments impacts the labour market, but this assumes that those participating are willing and able to work, if they were not otherwise excluded for being a retired senior or a person with a disability. This begs the question of how UBI addresses poverty when we exclude those who cannot work. This also suggests that there are conditions attached and therefore some programs do not meet the definition of a universal basic income. In short, the answer is that yes, we can have a universal basic income, but with caveats.

References

BIEN (n.d.). A short history of the basic income idea. Basic Income Earth Network. Retrieved from https://basicincome.org/history/

BIEN (n.d.). Bien: About basic income. Basic Income Earth Network. Retrieved from https://basicincome.org/about-basic-income/

Bernstien, J. (2021, September 19). What is basic income and which of Canada's main parties support it? | CBC News. CBC News. Retrieved from https://www.cbc.ca/news/canada-how-basic-income-works-1.6179760

Canada, S. (2022, August 2). Government of Canada. Questions and answers - Canada.ca. Retrieved from https://www.canada.ca/en/services/benefits/ei/cerb-application/questions.html

Cult MTL. (2021, December 22). 3 in 5 support universal basic income in Canada as high as $30K/year. Cult MTL. Retrieved from https://cultmtl.com/2021/12/3-in-5-canadians-supports-universal-basic-income-canada-as-high-as-30k-year-quebec/

Forget, E. L. (2011). The town with no poverty: The Health Effects of a Canadian Guaranteed annual income field experiment. Canadian Public Policy, 37(3), 283–305. doi: 10.3138/cpp.37.3.283

Green, D. A., Kesselman, J. R., & Tedds, L. M. (2021, January 28). Executive Summary: Covering All the Basics: Reforms for a More Just Society. BC Basic Income Panel. Retrieved from https://bcbasicincomepanel.ca/

Harper Collins Publishers Ltd. (n.d.). Labour supply definition and meaning: Collins English Dictionary. Collins English Dictionary. Retrieved from https://www.collinsdictionary.com/dictionary/english/labour-supply

Mendelson, M. (2019, October). Lessons from Ontario's basic income pilot. Maytree. Retrieved from https://maytree.com/publications/lessons-from-ontarios-basic-income-pilot/

Simpson, W., Mason, G., & Godwin, R. (2017). The Manitoba Basic Annual Income Experiment: Lessons Learned 40 Years Later. Canadian Public Policy 43(1), 85-104. Retrieved from https://www.muse.jhu.edu/article/651481.

Ward, L. (2021, March 10). The pros and cons of universal basic income. College of Arts and Sciences. Retrieved from https://college.unc.edu/2021/03/universal-basic-income/

Tax Reform for Billionaires

Introduction

There are 2,668 billionaires on Forbes' 36th-annual ranking of the planet's wealthiest people—87 fewer than a year ago. Billionaires are worth $12.7 trillion—$400 billion less than in 2021. The most dramatic drops have occurred in Russia, where there are 34 fewer billionaires than last year following Vladimir Putin's invasion of Ukraine. Also, a government crackdown on tech companies in China has led to 87 fewer Chinese billionaires on the list. (Dolan & Peterson-Withorn, 2022) The top five wealthiest people in 2022 are as follows:

- Elon Musk - Elon Musk cofounded six companies, including electric car maker Tesla.
- Jeff Bezos - founded e-commerce giant Amazon.
- Bernard Arnault oversees over 70 fashion and cosmetics brands, including Louis Vuitton.
- Bill Gates - founded Microsoft.
- Warren Buffet - successful investor.

The argumentive space between the left and right wings of the U.S. government and all other major economies is due to the massive stakes in tax reform for billionaires. For the left, taxing billionaires is an opportunity to move away from being so dependent on oil and gas revenue. The additional tax income may support a transition to renewable energy, with robust infrastructure designed to withstand climate change. Additional revenue would also support emergency social services, providing immediate relief through better funding for healthcare systems, emergency services, and social justice. For the right wing, taxing billionaires may be prudent. However, they should be done cautiously to avoid steering away potential investors. Federal, state, provincial, or municipal jurisdictions stand to lose tremendous prosperity if billionaires are turned off by too many taxes, too much government oversight, or a lack of affordable local labour.

In the following chapter, we will discuss general arguments for and against tax reform for billionaires. Details will include an examination of tax loopholes in Canada. A loophole is a technicality that allows a person or business to avoid the scope of a law or restriction without directly violating the law. When used within the context of taxes and their subsequent avoidance, loopholes provide ways for individuals and companies to remove income or assets from taxable situations into ones with lower taxes or none. (Hayes, 2022) In conclusion, we will examine the sociological implications of too much or insufficient taxation for billionaires.

Arguments for Taxing Billionaires

The question of how much billionaires should be taxed has been a focal point of the Joe Biden administration in the United States of America. President Biden's Billionaire Minimum Income Tax aims to make America's tax code fairer and reduce the deficit by about $360 billion within one decade. Through the Billionaire Minimum Income Tax and other measures, the President's goal is to reduce the budget deficit by another $1 trillion over the next decade. The Billionaire Minimum Income Tax will ensure that the very wealthiest Americans pay a tax rate of at least 20 percent on their total income, including unrealized appreciation. This minimum tax would ensure that the wealthiest Americans no longer pay a tax rate lower than teachers, firefighters, and other professionals. (White House, 2022) Supporters of the bill claim the legislation would raise $421.7 million in tax revenue. The nonpartisan Congressional Budget Office still needs to provide its independent estimate. Ilhan Abdullahi Omar, an American politician serving as the U.S. representative for Minnesota's 5th congressional district, made the following statement, "It is shameful that billionaires profit off the suffering of working families as the pandemic ravages the economy and kills thousands of Americans every day. For far too long, the richest 0.001% of America has avoided paying their fair share in taxes. This bill will go a long way towards addressing our nation's massive wealth inequality and finally guaranteeing healthcare as a human right."

Bernie Sanders, an American politician who has served as the junior United States senator from Vermont, stated, "At a time of enormous economic pain and suffering, we have a fundamental choice to make. We can continue to allow the very rich to get much richer while everyone else gets poorer and poorer. The legislation I am introducing today will tax the obscene wealth gains billionaires have made during this extraordinary crisis to guarantee healthcare as a right to all for an entire year. Or we can tax the winnings a handful of billionaires made during the pandemic to improve the health and well-being of tens of millions of Americans." (U.S. Congress, 2020)

Eventually, Biden would pass the Build Back Better Act in 2022. The BBBA imposed a straightforward tax on any taxpayer's adjusted gross income (AGI) beyond $10 million, with a rate of 5 percent, rising to 8 percent for AGI beyond $25 million. Some business groups did claim that this would be overly burdensome to those with incomes exceeding $10 million. The business groups called for carving out "pass-through" income, which is business profits that are not subject to the corporate income tax but instead included on the business owner's income tax returns. (Wamhoff, 2022) Tax reform for billionaires continues to be a significant issue for political parties on either side of the political spectrum, not only in the United States but elsewhere worldwide. The exact specifics of these tax reforms may vary drastically from country to country. Overall, the same themes of individualism vs. societal well-being are often discussed. Billionaires exist worldwide, regardless of what governments have formed. While some countries such as Russia and China tend to have more, shifting demographics will likely distribute more billionaires worldwide, requiring more significant tax reform if deemed necessary by local governments.

With much of the populace suffering from inflation, disease, and economic depression, some would likely argue that billionaires are too wealthy for their good and need to be taxed more, given their hedonistic and self-serving tendencies. Elon Musk closed a $44 billion deal to buy the social media site Twitter. He began by firing at least four top Twitter executives — including the chief executive and chief financial officer. The closing of the deal, which followed months of drama and legal challenges as Mr. Musk changed his mind about buying the company, sets Twitter on an uncertain course. (Conger & Hirsch, 2022) In a report entitled "The Toxic Tales of the 2022 Midterms", researchers at the Fletcher School at Tufts University said the early signs of Elon Musk's Twitter "show the platform is heading in the wrong direction under his leadership — at a particularly inconvenient time for American democracy." The researchers mention narratives about civil war, election fraud, citizen policing of voting, and allegations of child exploitation on Twitter from July through October since Elon Musk acquired Twitter. As more extremists and misinformation peddlers have tested the platform's boundaries, the researchers noted, "Post-Musk takeover, the quality of the conversation has decayed." (Digital Planet, 2022) There was even speculation that Elon Musk was purposefully devaluing Twitter due to its prominence among the left wing, journalists, and those critical of Elon Musk or his associated stakeholders. Elon Musk has since stated that he is expected to reduce his time at Twitter and eventually find a new leader to run the social media company. He hoped to complete an organizational restructuring. Tesla investors have a history of being concerned about the time Musk is devoted to Twitter and other business endeavours. (Jin et al., 2022)

In another move that was criticized by many, Jeff Bezos, CEO of Amazon, made a trip to space. His brother, Mark Bezos; Wally Funk, a storied aviator; and Oliver Daemen, an 18-year-old fresh out of high school, flew into near-orbit. Before this flight, Bezos's private space company, Blue Origin, had not flown its rocket with any people on board. By going first, Bezos wanted to prove that his vehicle was safe and that Blue Origin was finally ready to make its 11-minute suborbital trips an experience people could buy. (Koren, 2021) The acquisition of social media companies, and the apparent need to experience zero gravity, add more political impotence to bring about tax reforms against billionaires. While the exact motives of either Elon Musk or Jeff Bezos can be argued, it is apparent that these activities are not well received by those concerned with climate change, economic recession, weak education systems, degrading healthcare, and aging infrastructure. Amazon has been criticized for years over the conditions of its workers, with reports of staff urinating in bottles for fear of missing delivery rates and regularly working 14-hour days. Andy Levin, a U.S. representative from Michigan, pointed out the discrepancy between owner and worker in a tweet, "[t]omorrow, Jeff Bezos will ride around on a rocketship for a little over 10 minutes. Amazon warehouse workers on "megacycle" shifts will be on their feet for 10 hours. I'm fighting for an economy that values the dignity of their work, not the multiplication

154

of his wealth." (Gabbatt, 2021) Unfortunately for those advocating for tax reform for billionaires, powerful forces are at play working against their goals. In the next section, we will discuss the arguments against taxation and the potential reasons increases in tax may ultimately be detrimental to society.

Arguments Against Taxing Billionaires

The 16th Amendment expanded taxing power, allowing Congress to "lay and collect taxes on incomes, from whatever source derived." Opponents of the billionaire tax state that it is unconstitutional and that taxing unearned capital gains is problematic and will degrade the economy. John Delaney, a U.S. House of Representatives member from Maryland's 6th district, argued that the tax would likely result in legal challenges. That is because the tax would be "an actual tax on wealth" from capital gains rather than a tax on income from wealth, which is a mandated Congressional power under Article 1, Section 9 of the Constitution. Federal direct taxes are prohibited under the Constitution, barring income tax. (Henney, 2019) The practicability and reliability of such a tax would ultimately not be supported by the U.S. Senate.

During the lead-up to the U.S. 2022 midterm elections, Republicans were preparing to advance legislation that would make permanent the party's 2017 changes to the tax rates paid by individuals. Republican officials also push for scrapping specific tax increases on corporations designed to offset the cost of their enormous overall cut to the corporate tax rate. Many economists say the GOP's plans to expand the tax cuts fly against their promises to fight inflation and reduce the federal deficit, which have emerged as central themes of their 2022 midterm campaign rhetoric. Tax cuts boost inflation like new spending because they increase economic demand and throw it out of balance with supply. (Stein, 2022) The 2022 midterm elections resulted in the Democratic

Party barely managing to maintain the House, so these tax cuts did not occur. In 2017, when Trump's changes to the tax code—the most significant overhaul made in the last 30 years- were introduced, several vital factors limited the opposition to Trump's decision to decrease taxation for billionaires.

The law cut corporate tax rates permanently and individual tax rates temporarily. The highest earners were expected to benefit most from the law, while the lowest earners were believed to pay more in taxes once most individual tax provisions expire after 2025. The law created a single corporate tax rate of 21%. Unlike tax breaks for individuals, these provisions do not expire. Combined with state and local taxes, the statutory rate under the new law is 26.5%. That puts the U.S. below the weighted average for EU countries at 26.9%. Supporters of cutting the corporate tax rate argue it will reduce incentives for corporate inversions. Companies shift their tax base to low- or no-tax jurisdictions, often through mergers with foreign firms. In its finalized form, however, the TCJA cut the corporate tax rate, benefiting shareholders—who tend to be higher earners. It only cuts individuals' taxes for a limited time. It scales back estate tax and reduces the taxes levied on pass-through income (70% of which goes to the highest-earning 1%). It does not close the carried interest loophole, which benefits professional investors. These conditions are likely to benefit high earners disproportionately. (Floyd, 2022)

The arguments against tax reform for billionaires also exist in Canada. Canadian billionaire Jim Pattison warned that recent policy proposals to tax the wealthy might lead to investment fleeing Canada and make it harder to tackle current labour shortages. Pattison argues that encouraging investment will create jobs needed to help ensure Canada's economy, with a subsequent strong recovery from the COVID-19 pandemic. Pattison said that tackling the current labour shortage across several industries, notably in manufacturing, may ease inflation that has seen the price of goods ranging from automobiles to food spike in recent months. (George-Cosh, 2021)

Effects on Society

Having some much money, investment capital, and, ultimately, political or societal sway possessed by individual humans may be problematic. Millions of people use Twitter daily to share what they think and read, making the service a global water cooler for everything from politics to sports. Nevertheless, Twitter is also a den of misinformation and harassment that the company's executives regularly condemn, though they have not fully addressed. As a business, Twitter's track record is mixed. The considerable influence of its service on public discourse has yet to translate into a fast-growing company like many of its tech-focused peers. (Fortune Staff, 2022) The impact of Elon Musk resulted in financial consequences for Twitter and Elon himself, with questionable results and an uncertain future at the company. For many, the resulting uncertainty at Twitter is justification that billionaires should be taxed more and that any individual should not be able to purchase a large, influential company like Twitter as if it were a luxury item.

In the wake of the U.S. tax reform, there has been much discussion about how Canada's tax system stacks up. Moreover, while there are some key differences, it is clear that our system is also in need of reform. For example, consider the treatment of billionaires in Canada. As of August 2022, David Thomson was the wealthiest man in Canada, with an estimated net worth of $51 billion U.S. dollars, followed by Changpeng Zhao with $17 billion. Jim Pattison is worth $12 billion. David Cheriton has The net worth of David Cheriton and Anthony Von Mandl is over $9 billion each. (Ireland, 2022) Under our current plan, they can pay as little as 15% of their income, thanks to a loophole known as the "loophole rate." The loophole rate is significantly lower than regular Canadians' top marginal tax rate, which is currently 29%. This discrepancy is unfair and needs to be addressed. We should ask billionaires to pay their fair share, just like everyone else. A solution may exist with a new tax bracket for billionaires, with a rate of 35%.

A new tax bracket would ensure that everyone pays a more equitable share, helping to reduce inequality in Canada. Closing these loopholes is possible and, in many cases, simple, but politicians have been reluctant to act due in part to lobbying by special interests. Public pressure can push financial stakeholders to adopt the needed changes in tax laws and recover billions required to support public services. In total, Canada's tax loopholes cost the federal government over $40 billion per year. (Explainer Staff, 2022) With the cost of social services, climate mitigation, and economic stimulus expected to grow, the tolerance towards tax loopholes and lack of political will to create tax reform will decrease. A 1% tax on wealth over $20 million in Canada would generate about $10 billion in revenue in its first year. Would Canadian billionaires flee the country to avoid a wealth tax? Some may, but a well-designed wealth tax will only allow them to dodge their tax obligations if they face financial penalties. A steep "exit tax" can be applied to expatriation to recognize Canadian society's contributions to these fortunes. Exit tax rates are set at 40% of have been proposed, which could be even higher to discourage the use of loopholes. (Hemingway, 2021) Canada is home to many billionaires thanks to its robust industries, especially within the oil & gas sector.

Conclusion

As austerity measures continue to expand worldwide, the appetite for tolerating billionaires within society is decreasing. Elon Musk's $44 billion acquisition of Twitter shines a light on the effectuation of billionaires upon democratic society. While it is still too early to say definitively how much money billionaires and millionaires will save in response to tax reform, it is clear that they stand to gain a lot from these changes. So far, most of the benefits have gone to those already doing very well financially, which is not correct or fair. Some may argue that this is fair since billionaires have worked hard to earn their money and should be able to keep as much of it as possible. Some will say that tax reform for billionaires will hurt investment and economic growth. Tax reform for billionaires could have the opposite effect by encouraging more investment in Canada from wealthy individuals and families who want to take advantage of our favourable tax rates.

There are many arguments against tax reform for billionaires. It could harm the economy. It would benefit governments that are liberal with their spending more than the middle class or poor. Furthermore, it would not create jobs. However, there are also good reasons to support tax reform for billionaires. It would help reduce the deficit while also funding climate mitigation efforts. Another is that it would make it easier for small businesses to create jobs while in competition with giant corporations such as Amazon. A third reason is that it would help stimulate the economy with an increased potential for stimulus spending by governments. There are many different ways to design tax reform for billionaires. One option is to increase the taxes on capital gains and dividends. Another option is to reduce the number of loopholes that allow the wealthy to avoid paying taxes. A third option is to impose a surtax on millionaires and billionaires. What may be lacking is the political will to implement such measures.

References

Conger, K., & Hirsch, L. (2022, October 27). Elon Musk Completes $44 Billion Deal to Own Twitter. nytimes.com. Retrieved from https://www.nytimes.com/2022/10/27/technology/elon-musk-twitter-deal-complete.html

Digital Planet. (2022, November 14). The Toxic Tales of the 2022 Midterms: Unraveling the Lies, Hate, and Extremism Polluting the Public Square. https://sites.tufts.edu/. Retrieved from https://sites.tufts.edu/digitalplanet/the-toxic-tales-of-the-2022-midterms-unraveling-the-lies-hate-and-extremism-polluting-the-public-square/

Dolan, K., & Peterson-Withorn, C. (2022). World's Billionaires List. Forbes. Retrieved from https://www.forbes.com/billionaires/

Explainer Staff. (2022). Explainer: What are Canada's worst tax loopholes? https://www.taxfairness.ca/. Retrieved from https://www.taxfairness.ca/en/resources/explainers/explainer-what-are-canadas-worst-tax-loopholes

Floyd, D. (2022, April 30). Explaining the Trump Tax Reform Plan. https://www.investopedia.com/. Retrieved from https://www.investopedia.com/taxes/trumps-tax-reform-plan-explained/

Fortune Staff. (2022, November 1). Twitter. Fortune. Retrieved from https://fortune.com/company/twitter/

Gabbatt, A. (2021, July 20). Bezos blasted for traveling to space while Amazon workers toil on planet Earth. The Guardian. Retrieved from https://www.theguardian.com/science/2021/jul/20/bezos-space-travel-blue-origin-amazon-criticism

George-Cosh, D. (2021, September 16). Jim Pattison warns wealth tax will lead to Canadian capital exodus - BNN Bloomberg. BNN. Retrieved from https://www.bnnbloomberg.ca/jim-pattison-warns-taxing-the-rich-will-lead-to-canadian-capital-exodus-1.1653262

Hayes, A. (2022, April 18). Loophole. Investopedia. Retrieved from https://www.investopedia.com/terms/l/loophole.asp

Hemingway, A. (2021, March 11). Wealth tax would raise far more money than previously thought. Policy Note. Retrieved from https://www.policynote.ca/tax-the-rich/

Henney, M. (2019, August 14). John Delaney slams 2020 Democrats' wealth tax proposals as unconstitutional. Fox Business. Retrieved from https://www.foxbusiness.com/politics/john-delaney-wealth-tax-unconstitutional

House, T. W. (2022, March 28). President's Budget Rewards Work, Not Wealth with new Billionaire Minimum Income Tax. The White House. Retrieved from https://www.whitehouse.gov/omb/briefing-room/2022/03/28/presidents-budget-rewards-work-not-wealth-with-new-billionaire-minimum-income-tax/

Ireland, S. (2022, September 7). Wealthiest People in Canada (September 6, 2022). CEOWORLD Magazine. Retrieved from https://ceoworld.biz/2022/09/07/wealthiest-people-in-canada-september-6-2022/

Jin, H., Hals, T., & Hals, T. (2022, November 17). Elon Musk says he will find a new leader for Twitter. Reuters. Retrieved from https://www.reuters.com/technology/elon-musk-says-he-expects-reduce-his-time-twitter-court-testimony-2022-11-16/

Koren, M. (2021, July 21). Jeff Bezos Really Flew to Space. The Atlantic. Retrieved from https://www.theatlantic.com/science/archive/2021/07/jeff-bezos-blue-origin-successful-flight/619484/

Stein, J. (2022, October 17). GOP wants to push to extend Trump tax cuts after midterm elections. Washington Post. Retrieved from https://www.washingtonpost.com/us-policy/2022/10/17/republicans-tax-trump-biden/

U.S. Congress. (2020, October 23). Summary of S. 4490 (116th): Make Billionaires Pay Act. GovTrack. Retrieved from https://www.govtrack.us/congress/bills/116/s4490/summary

Wamhoff, S. (2022, June). No Reason to Water Down the Tax Reforms in the Build Back Better Act. Institute on Taxation and Economic Policy. Retrieved from https://itep.org/no-reason-to-water-down-the-tax-reforms-in-the-build-back-better-act/

The Law and Economics of Redistribution

What is the economics of redistribution? It is the income and wealth that is transferred, including physical properties from some individuals to others through a social mechanism such as taxation, welfare, public services, land reform, monetary policies, confiscation, divorce, or tort. Now the question is: should legal rules be used to address income inequality?

A legal rule or law is something that has been officially approved by the state's legislative body. Legal rules are usually taken upon the court to decide cases being brought before them and may impose sanctions on those who choose to violate the rule. The matter of inequality in income between the rich and poor should come up in conversation as a legal rule that should be passed down and approved by the court for equality incomes between the rich and poor in how the money is distributed and doesn't cause distortion within society that is efficient and productive. Dermick's (2016) journal found the following:

A widely-held view argues only the tax system and not the legal system should be used for the redistribution of income. While this argument comes from a variety of normative statements and has support across the political spectrum, there is also well-known law and economics version. This argument, known as the "Double-Distortion" argument, is simply stated. Legal rules that redistribute income only add to the economic distortions that are already present in the tax system. It would therefore be better for everyone, and especially the poor, to instead adopt an efficient, non-redistribution legal rule, and increase redistribution through the tax system. (p.1).

This would be very much beneficial for the poor if the redistribution runs through the tax system it would increase income. This is a more efficient and non-distribution legal rule system to help them and make them more equal as well. According to Dermick, this is indicative of how exclusively mixing legal rules and taxation is the best manner of addressing economic inequality. (2016, p. 1). Kaplan's (2003) article found the following:

The rising of economic inequality in recent years has been growing awareness that the gap between rich and poor In America is increasing. Whether measured in terms of annual income, percentage of financial assets owned, or the earnings of corporate executives compared to ordinary workers, the incontrovertible evidence shows that more and more economic resources are controlled by fewer and fewer people (para. 5).

Weisbach's (2003) article found the following:

Consider a legal rule that redistributes income by varying from the efficient result. The legal rule redistributes income, which is good. It also creates inefficiencies. Because it redistributes, it reduces the return from working and therefore causes labor/leisure distortions (p. 447).

The rich are getting richer while almost everybody is either stationary or diminishing. Dermick's (2016) journal found the following:

Within economics, redistribution is defined simply as a reduction in inequality. Consistent with this definition, it is possible for a redistributive legal change to be either inefficient or efficient since a legal shift that meets such a condition both reduces inequality and is not only non-distortionary but increases wealth, unmistakeable superior to redistribution through the tax and transfer system, which is always distortionary (p.4).

Indeed, Dermick follows by stating that:

More importantly, under the typical optimal tax policy, a high level of inequality will justify a higher level of tax distortions. Therefore, given legal rule that has accomplished a certain amount of redistribution and produces a certain level of inefficiency is more likely to dominate the optimal tax policies when equality is higher. The same conclusion obtains when we hold the level of inequality constant but vary our judgment about it. If the public or policymakers become less tolerant of inequality, more significant tax distortion can be justified. But then because of these more significant distortions, it is more likely that a particular redistributive legal rule will constitute a more efficient alternative. Like so, redistributive legal rules, even if inefficient, are more likely to be superior to taxes and transfers precisely when inequality is a more serious concern (p.5, 2016).

Problems of this come up in Canada as well with rising concerns about income inequality in recent years. A lot can still be learned about the economic forces driving the distribution of earning income in this country and how they might evolve in the coming years. The Institute for Research on Public Policy collaborated with the Canadian Labour Market and Skills Researcher Network to gather information and evidence on the causes and effects of rising income inequality in Canada and others consider the role of policy. They analyzed comprehensive reviews of inequality showing the trends in the recent decade of changing earning and income dynamics among middle-class and top earners, wages, job polarization across provinces, and persistent poverty among vulnerable groups. They believe that the changing role of education has a part to play as well explaining these trends and also the complex interplay of redistributive policies and politics. Recent data shows that income inequality in Canada increased substantially during the 1980s and the first half of the 1990s but has been relatively stable in the past 25 years. The people who felt this hit the most when the income earners and younger people, while the older people were benefiting from higher retirement income. United states income inequality is still higher than in Canada for the last four decades, with the main difference observed at the high end of the income distribution.

The COVID-19 pandemic in Canada had amplified the economic gap between the rich and the poor and further marginalized racialized individuals and women. Reports of household economics present key indicators about the financial well-being of Canadians that evolved during the pandemic. Low-income households saw a rise in income of almost 37 per cent over the first quarter of 2020. Young households recorded the greatest gain in their net worth. In consequence, the gap between the incomes of the lowest and higher earners dropped in 2020 as economics recuperated in the third quarter. Higher earners coupled with lower spending due to lockdowns brought about unprecedented gains in net worth. There were other reports in gain as well. Wealth for the lowest-income bracket grew the most, owing to surges in the value of their real estate holding. Hiding growing inequalities between employed and those facing dwindling financial security. Governments trying to create an appropriate mix of policies for the recovery stages of the pandemic. There are so many families in Canada who are coping with the COVID-19 economy.

All across the world, the pandemic hit them hard and inequality in income became more and more of an issue even more so in the states. Established trends of growing inequality may continue roughly as before, involving new technologies, international trade, and the growth of "superstar" firms. Employment, earnings, and schooling were affected differently across demographic groups and occupations. The pandemic disrupted lower-paid, service sector employment most, disadvantaging women and lower-income groups at least temporarily, and this may have scarring effects (Piacentini et al., 2022)

With COVID-19 still going on, the pandemic has exacerbated global income inequality, partly reversing the previous two decades. Recoveries in emerging markets and developing economies ("EMDEs") are weak which results in expected rising between-country inequality. Within-country income inequality is also estimated to have increased somewhat in EMDEs because of severe job and income losses among lower-income population groups. If we were to reverse the increase in income inequality we would need to reduce between-country and within-country inequality with the support of the global community. The pandemic jeopardized the progress made in reducing global income inequality achieved in the previous two decades. Noted in the 2008-10 global financial crisis, the deep recession caused by the pandemic is lagging the economic recovery in EMDEs compared with advanced economics and has raised between-country income inequality. The increases in within-country inequality reflected severe job and income losses among low-skilled workers, low-income households, informal workers, and women. There is the risk of income inequality increasing in the long run which is high inflation and public debt levels may be a problem for countries' ability to support vulnerable groups and facilitate recovery and sustainable growth. A comprehensive strategy is needed to steer the global economy onto a more inclusive developed path.

The question we need to start asking is how much of the law, whether it is public or not is regulated solely by the principles of justice that focus on the distribution of basic liberties, economic resources, and opportunities. (Scheffler, 2015) We need to start asking these questions how the law is going to benefit the people, and how justice is being played out in terms of our economic resources and opportunities given to us?

Income and poverty rates differ widely among and within specific categories of people such as sex, age, race, and nation. With the gap between the income and poverty rates, something that is often brought up is income inequality, and not long after that income distribution. When there is income distribution, it is exactly as it sounds: income is redistributed throughout society to lessen the income inequality present. Consider Grundler and Schuermeyer's (2017) journal findings:

Evidence from a large panel of harmonized data highlights the negative effect of income inequality on economic growth. Less equal societies tend to have less educated populations, higher fertility rates, and lower investment shares. These effects are particularly prevalent if credit availability is limited, while public education spending attenuates the negative effects of inequality. Public redistribution, measured as the difference between Ginis of the market and net income hampers growth via lower investment and increased fertility. Yet, combined with its positive effect through lower inequality, the impact of redistribution is insignificant. In developing countries redistribution can even be Growth-enhancing. (para. 1)

Income redistribution aims to promote economic stability and possibilities for society's less prosperous members (narrowing the gap between the poor and the wealthy), and so frequently includes financing for social services. These services are paid in taxes, and people who advocate for income redistribution claim that higher taxes for the richer members of society are necessary to best support public programs benefiting those who are underprivileged. Regarding this, Glaeser et al. (2002) contend that:

In many countries, the operation of legal, political, and regulatory institutions is subverted by the wealthy and the politically powerful for their benefit. This subversion takes the form of corruption, intimidation, and other forms of influence. We present a model of such institutional subversion—focusing

168

specifically on courts—and on the effects of inequality in economic and political resources on the magnitude of subversion. We then use the model to analyze the consequences of institutional subversion for the law and order environment in the country, as well as capital accumulation and growth. (para. 1)

Taxation and income transfers to the poorest segment of society are the most direct way to keep inequality in check and reduce poverty in the short term. These instruments are particularly appropriate when the benefits of growth fail to reach the poor. But most of the time they are too small to make a difference. On average, taxes on personal income and cash benefits to the poor are almost 10 times lower, as the proportion of GDP, than in advanced economies. The conditional cash transfer program has been successful in demonstrating that it is possible to transfer cash efficiently to the poor in developing economies. This program will transfer money to households with a condition that complies with certain pre-defined requirements like up-to-date vaccinations or regular school attendance by children. Programs like that should continue to improve in the future with the advancing information of technology, particularly the use of mobile phones.

The current impact on poverty and inequality is limited. If we were to expand these programs we would require more resources to do so. A higher and more effective income tax in the upper part of the income scale could help raise necessary funds. So generalized use of bank accounts, credit cards, and debit cards by higher-income people in most countries should make it easier to monitor personal incomes and reduce tax evasion. Political economy issues aside, this should lead developing economies' governments to be more emphasis on direct taxation than they already do. There are strong cases for the expansion of redistribution in developing economies where growth is satisfactory but poverty reduction is low. Of course, there are political obstacles to doing this but also challenges related to the country's administrative capacity.

Income distribution is an issue that cannot be ignored in the people-centered development philosophy, serving as an essential means to narrow the income gap and achieve common prosperity. According to the tenth meeting of the Central Committee for Financial and Economic Affairs held on August 17, 2021, "[w]e should adhere to the concept of people-centered development, promote common prosperity through high-quality development, correctly handle the relationship between efficiency and equity, conduct institutional arrangements for primary distribution, redistribution and tertiary distribution, and intensify efforts to regulate taxation, social security, and transfer payment". Personal income tax is an important redistributive instrument with the function of reducing income disparity (Yue et al., 2014).

If done properly, income redistribution can lower poverty by reducing inequality. But it may not speed up the process of growth in any major way, except perhaps reducing social tension arisings of imbalance, allowing the poor to devote more resources to human physical asset accumulation. Directly investing in opportunities for poor people is essential. Not only the transfer to the poor should consist of mere cash but should increase people's capacity to generate income today and in the future to come. Education and training as well as access to health care, micro-credit, water, energy, and transportation are powerful instruments. The need for social assistance is vital to help prevent people from falling into poverty traps and shock hits. Conditional cash transfer is shown to motivate families in sending their children to school, improve their nutrition and monitor their health. But families need to meet the additional demands of the facilities to be financed.

Strategies that can promote more equality and greater growth focus on gradually increasing resources and allocating them to services that will support the poorest sections of the community in this or the future generation. We need other approaches that don't depend too much on redistribution that might accomplish similar results. However, prior to considering redistribution, the governments should explore more on improving pro-poor aspects and or inclusivity of their economic growth strategy, particularly through increasing employment for unskilled individuals. Having the law that dictates and sets the minimum wages, while controversial due to the possible negative effects if the minimum wages get too high, results in more fairness regarding the distribution of wages. Such initiatives may genuinely enhance labour productivity in undeveloped economies. Anti-discrimination laws can also promote equality and foster growth by reducing inequality and ensuring that growth by improving work and training incentives for minority groups. Also anti-corruption strategies, by reducing rent-seeking, are probably the best candidates for both enhancing growth and income equality, even if the inequality arising from corruption is then difficult to observe. Per Nussim (2007):

Many legal scholars believe that equity should be considered in designing legal rules. Kaplow and Shavell (1994) seriously challenged this approach. They proved that the tax-transfer system is superior to legal rules in redistributing wealth. This paper reexamines their 'double distortion' claim, presenting two main arguments. The first shows that the 'double distortion' claim is not necessarily valid under welfarism. In particular, under an ex-post approach to welfarism, which generally implies that society pays attention to the ex-post (actual) rather than expected redistribution, the proof of the tax superiority breaks down. Secondly, and more importantly, it is proven that, in principle, tort rules can easily be designed to circumvent 'double distortion' effects. Thus, the tort system is not inherently more inefficient than the tax-transfer system in accomplishing redistribution. The paper generally concludes that although there are often no good reasons for redistribution within the legal system, theoretically and a priori it is not an inferior redistribution mechanism.

In the end, it is up to the governments to choose their preferred policy combination. The choice is quite difficult since some parties will necessarily lose in the short run and might not make up for their losses anytime soon. But we do have available instruments that would benefit all in the long run, through faster growth, more rapid poverty reduction, and less inequality. It would be a serious mistake not to use them.

There are both benefits and contras to redistribution. The benefits of redistribution include the reduction of socioeconomic disparities. It also has a broader impact on the economy as a whole, rather than just a few individuals, even those who don't work or can't work are guaranteed to have a way to support themselves enough to survive, it can assist in bridging the wealth gap in nations with gap inequality when political and social conflicts or the emergence of populist regimes may be detrimental to long-term economic growth, the incentive to work hard motivates people to work hard to get more money, helps avoid the destruction of economic equality, and personal freedom and economic inequality ensure empowered through a free enterprise system that helps them earn success through their potential.

The contras of having redistribution are, even if the unprivileged gain more access to funds, these individuals continue to lack the necessary skills, ambitions, and relationships to compete successfully in the economy, state and municipal taxes tend to be regressive, meaning that individuals with lower incomes end up giving a larger percentage of their income than those with higher incomes since the poor have to pay higher taxes if they work, they lose out on a large part of their redistribution of money or funds. This in turn penalizes them from working and makes them more dependent on the funds given, social problems are causing friction attributed to inequality like more people participating in riots, also increased crime rates show inequalities act as an incentive to commit a crime to gain more, higher prices to consumers show the result in unfair distribution of income between suppliers and consumers, and division

172

in society, income inequality results in the division between the poor and the wealthy. The poor only associate with the poor people and the wealthy people talk to other wealthy people.

References

Dimick, M. (2016). Should the law do anything about economic inequality? Cornell Journal of Law and Public Policy, 26(1), 1-69. Retrieved from https://scholarship.law.cornell.edu/cgi/viewcontent.cgi?article=1444&context=cjlpp

Fischel, D. R. (1998). Lawyers and confidentiality. The University of Chicago Law Review, 65(1), 1-33. Retrieved from https://chicagounbound.uchicago.edu/cgi/viewcontent.cgi?article=2413&context=journal_articles

Glaeser, E., Scheinkman, J., & Shleifera, A. (2002, December 31). The Injustice of Inequality. Journal of Monetary Economics, 50(1), 199-222. doi: 10.1016/S0304-3932(02)00204-0

Gründler, K. & Scheuermeyer, P. (2017). Growth effects of inequality and redistribution: What are the transmission channels? Journal of Macroeconomics, 55(1), 293-313. doi: 10.1016/j.jmacro.2017.12.001

Kaplan, R. L. (2003). Economic inequality and the role of law. Michigan Law Review, 101(6), 1987-2006. Retrieved from https://repository.law.umich.edu/cgi/viewcontent.cgi?params=/context/mlr/article/1862/&path_info=

Nussim, J. (2007, October 26). Redistribution mechanisms. Review of Law & Economics, 3(2), 323-341. doi: /10.2202/1555-5879.1161/html

Piacentini, J. (2022). The impact of COVID-19 on labor markets and inequality. U.S. Bureau of Labor Statistics. Retrieved from https://www.bls.gov/osmr/research-papers/2022/ec220060.htm

Scheffler, S. (2015). Distributive Justice, the Basic Structure and the Place of Private Law. Oxford Journal of Legal Studies, 35(2), 213-235. doi: org/10.1093/ojls/gqu030

Zhang, X., & Yue, X. (2022, July 1). A study on the income redistribution effect of China's 2018 personal income tax reform. China Finance and Economic Review, 11(1), 70-87. doi: org/10.1515/cfer-2022-0004

Conclusion

We have covered many topics, from tax equity to private property, economic schools of thought, taxation for specific demographics, tax evasion or tax loopholes, and specific consideration towards tax reform, universal basic income, and other concepts. This book is by no means an exhaustive examination of taxation, which is a voluminous task. Instead, we have focused on specific topics to give readers a better understanding of taxes, leading to more effective decision-making and more organizational objectives being met. Tax reform is becoming an increasingly political issue, attracting attention like never before among citizens and governments, with an increased influence from social media. Taxation is an essential consideration during business negotiations or regarding strategic transformational decisions.

The world is constantly changing with geopolitical shifts, technological inventions, changing consumer demands, and the emergence of new companies, for example, Twitter or Facebook. Companies that meet compliance obligations while meeting strategic goals add value to their organizations. Future leaders face unique challenges as they encounter an ever-changing taxation environment. Companies that fail to do so may lead themselves towards punitive measures, perhaps resulting in business failure and insolvency. For individuals, awareness of taxation is critical to daily life, culminating in yearly tax returns. Some of these people may become millionaires and billionaires, with incredible sway and influence over taxation policy, with inherent expertise at exploiting tax loopholes. The decisions made on tax reform reflect politicians' inclinations to either lean towards the left, resulting in higher tax rates, or, conversely, move towards the right, resulting in more tax cuts for the wealthiest humans on planet Earth. Both sides of the political aisle may argue that their methods result in a just society. Precisely what tax structure society may ultimately possess is still uncertain.